BREAKTHROUGH BOOKS

BALBOA

DISCOVERER OF
THE PACIFIC

VASCO NUÑEZ DE BALBOA

A BREAKTHROUGH
BOOK

BALBOA

DISCOVERER OF THE PACIFIC

by Jeannette Mirsky

Edited by Walter Lord

PICTURES BY HANS GUGGENHEIM

HARPER & ROW, PUBLISHERS
NEW YORK, EVANSTON, AND LONDON

To my hosts at the Villa Serbelloni:
in Bellagio and New York City

Contents

Illustrations

BALBOA

DISCOVERER OF
THE PACIFIC

1
The Beginning

Balboa's name is known to everyone. He has thus won the final victory over his enemies, who cunningly cast a veil of silence over his name to hide their terrible deed.

As an explorer, Vasco Nuñez de Balboa—to give him his full, sonorous Spanish name—was like a rocket that darted upward, for his memorable cascade of achievements illuminated the unknown New World. His work was accomplished in the brief years after Columbus's four voyages (1492–1502) and before Cortés's conquest of Mexico (1519–1521). The brilliance cast by Columbus and Cortés did not dim Balboa's light. An empty firmament awaited the host of explorers whose stellar exploits now adorn it. Among those who pushed back the horizons and matched men's hopes with their discoveries, one of the most notable was Balboa. Just as Columbus crossed the pathless Atlantic to give Europeans a New World, so Balboa made his way across the land to give them a new ocean. Discoverer of the Pacific, he invented the method used by explorers of all nations who penetrated the vastness of the Americas; conqueror of the Isthmus of Panama, he made friends of his defeated Indian enemies.

This, then, is the story of Balboa's grandeur and success and why and how it was tragically shadowed by mean motives and envy, by the ambitions of influential courtiers and the vengeance of petty schemers. A brave man and wise, a gifted and honorable leader, Balboa could guard against death from poisoned arrows but not from poisonous tongues. We shall see how the man who mastered a hostile wilderness became lost in a jungle of intrigue.

Intrigue, marked by lying accusations, connivings, and betrayals, is most ferocious when the stakes are high and the circumstances unusual and unsettled. Such conditions existed during the years immediately following 1492—the year the Spaniards had completed winning their country back from the Moors and the year Columbus gave them a new world to conquer.

Their Catholic Majesties Ferdinand and Isabella were suddenly faced with a host of problems, each important, each pressing for solution. How was this unexpected acquisition to be explored and colonized, administered and exploited? True, in 1492 the capture of Granada, the Moors' last stronghold, had unified and brought peace to Spain; this gave Ferdinand and Isabella more time to attend to the overseas situation. Capable rulers, they considered how best to insure order in a domain so distant and how to create laws and agencies to handle a region whose size and worth were unknown. Ruling was their business. They knew that order in a realm promoted prosperity, a policy they maintained even in the face of the sickening spectacle of Columbus brought home from his third voyage in chains. Serious dissatisfaction in Hispaniola had made it clear how unfitted the Admiral of the Ocean Sea was to govern the colony. This was why Ferdinand and Isabella did not hesitate to deprive him of his right, as set forth in his contract with them, to be viceroy and governor-general of all new lands, and to replace him with an able administrator, Don Francisco de Bobadilla. And later, after Columbus's death, his son Don Diego Colón had to show his ability to govern, before the Crown honored his inherited right to the governorship of Hispaniola.

The task of the Spanish rulers in planting colonies overseas was as novel as the New World itself. Neither custom nor tradition could help them, there being nothing comparable in Europe's past to guide them. And so the Spanish rulers moved slowly, warily, letting time and events reveal men's motives and capabilities. Hand in hand with the explorers the Spanish government ventured into new territories.

The two ventures—extending the frontier and administrating a frontier empire—though separated by the Atlantic and utterly different in essence, were intimately joined. Repeatedly the situation on one side of the ocean affected that on the other. Together they form the incredible Spanish adventure which brought out the best and the worst qualities in the main actors.

It is pleasant to relate the best qualities: the daring of navigators and explorers—the famous names and the unnamed hundreds who formed the crews and land parties; the conscience of devoted churchmen and administrators; and the awe and wonder, sadness and pity, which moved some to set down in words the white man's coming. Much was laudable and much more was inspiring as the Spaniards mobilized their strength and spirit and mind to answer so great a challenge.

It is also necessary to remember that the self-interest which sustained the brave and daring made the ambitious easily corruptible and ready to join in conspiracy. The most honorable and successful were never free from suspicion or safe from jealousy. Ugly deeds were done secretly, in the dark. They too are part of the story.

With the end of the *reconquista,* as the Christian recovery of Spain was called, hundreds of tough, brave fighting men were left with nothing to do and no place to go. The New World offered them both. Every man who had a sword could carve out a career. Every man who had a little money could make a fortune. Every man who had influential friends could make himself powerful. Younger sons of noblemen and peasants, poor and well-to-do, soldiers, priests, courtiers, and lawyers—men from all walks of life—crossed the Atlantic to the settlement of Santo Domingo on the island of Hispaniola.

Hispaniola was the Spanish name for the island where Haiti and the Dominican Republic are now located. The town of Santo Domingo, founded in 1496, was where the governor lived. The island was like a funnel through which the first fighters and settlers poured into the New World and quickly spread to the other islands—Cuba, Jamaica, Puerto Rico, Trinidad, Martinique, and the many smaller islands of the Caribbean. Hispaniola was Spain's foothold in the New World from which the conquistadores fanned out to fight for Christ, for Their Catholic Majesties Ferdinand and Isabella, and for their own profit.

Men crowded the ships bound for the New World. Luckily they sought treasure and adventure, not ease. America was neither gentle nor kind. The seas around Hispaniola were perilous. Monstrous hurricanes, which had their birth there, smashed whole fleets; villainous waves swallowed up men and animals, provisions and supplies. Reefs and sandbars trapped unwary ships; and the *broma*, the termite-like sea worm that can turn the stoutest timbers into Swiss cheese, sank their unprotected ships. Nor was life more certain once they reached land. Many men died slowly of starvation. Many more fell into debt and were hopelessly tied to Santo Domingo, for debtors were forbidden by law to leave the island. Many newcomers died quickly of fevers and many were killed fighting the Indians. And still they came. For every ship that foundered, twenty new ones sailed for the New World. For every man who died, twenty new arrivals took his place. No one thought of death but only of the rich prizes to be grabbed—somewhere.

By 1509, when most of the Caribbean islands had been explored and colonized, the land to the west became the next target for exploration and settlement.

What lay beyond the island of Hispaniola? Columbus had traced a coast that extended for hundreds of miles. Was it another, larger island? So Columbus thought as he probed its coast to find a waterway around it. Other ships had extended his vain search along the coastline. Were they finished with finding islands and had they reached the mainland? Anything was possible and every hope, because nothing was known. This was the frontier. To the Spaniards the word meant gold, pearls, and precious stones, fine estates and titles to match.

Wherever men gathered together, their talk always returned to the same subject: the fabulous cargo brought from the Pearl Coast of the mainland by Peralonso Niño and Rodrigo de Bastidas eight years before. Niño and Bastidas! Fortune had favored them. They had been licensed by the Crown to seek the pearls which Columbus had seen some Indians wearing. Still intent on finding the waterway to the East, he had been too busy to locate the source of these pearls.

Don Rodrigo de Bastidas, a lawyer, one of the early treasure hunters, had explored the Pearl Coast, as the region from Venezuela to Panama was then called, and found the waters where the Indians dived for pearls. Not only had he found treasure and survived the hazards of lands and seas and savages, he had had to defend his actions before the suspicious Don Francisco de Bobadilla. Don Francisco was the newly appointed governor sent to Hispaniola to suppress lawlessness—illegal treasure-seeking and slave-hunting—and restore order on the frontier. Even the great Columbus had been deprived of his authority. Clearance by the man who had sent Columbus home in chains made Don Rodrigo a hero, for he had been permitted to return to Spain, keeping all of his huge fortune.

The treasure amassed by his expedition Don Rodrigo kept wholly for himself. He did not share even a small part with the men who had sailed with him and with him suffered shipwreck and hunger. These men had returned to Santo Domingo as poor as when they had started. Among them was young Balboa. Tall and well-built, conspicuous for his red hair, he was respected for his strength and swordsmanship. He was pointed out to new arrivals as one of the survivors, one of the veterans, of that treasure hunt. He had seen and handled the riches of the New World—something few young men had done. He had experienced the dangers visible and invisible of strange lands and people. Of all this he never wearied telling—he respected the eager curiosity of those who might lose their lives in search of treasure.

To no one did Balboa mention the valuable information he had gained on that early voyage under Bastidas. Not even to his closest friends would he reveal the life-and-death knowledge of Indian customs he had acquired. Now and then he mentioned the bitterness felt by the men who had served Don Rodrigo, the resentment they all had for the lawyer's greed.

Don Rodrigo went home to enjoy his wealth. Balboa remained in Santo Domingo, the richer only for two lessons he had learned on that expedition: a useful, precious bit of information and a hatred of greed and injustice. Still young, he settled down to wait for the expedition which would give him the chance to capitalize on his special, hard-won knowledge. It could, he knew, become the keystone in an arch of fame and fortune.

To keep from starving while he awaited this chance, he hired out his fighting skill to men who had been favored with grants of land. They still had need to "pacify" the Indians, as the Spaniards called their taking over of island after island, successfully pitting gunpowder and steel swords against armies of Indians fighting with bone-tipped arrows and fire-hardened wooden spears. But even this kind of work did not save Balboa from having to sell everything he owned. Finally, when he had nothing left but the clothes he wore, the sword he carried, and his dog, Leoncico, he fell into debt.

II
The Stowaway

Vasco Nuñez de Balboa was thirty-four and hopelessly in debt when he left Santo Domingo as a stowaway. It was risky, for the law was very severe on runaway debtors, but it was his only way of taking the opportunity for which he had been waiting. He had had plenty of time to perfect his plan, and he had loyal friends to help him. Men trusted him for his experience, for his fighting skill and self-assurance, for his reasonable and pleasant nature. His company was always welcome.

Eight years after Don Rodrigo had been permitted to seek out the Pearl Coast, King Ferdinand authorized new expeditions to colonize the Caribbean side of the Isthmus of Panama. Ferdinand, now ruling alone since his wife's death, was unwilling to give so large and rich a prize to one man: he divided the coast between Alonso de Ojeda and Diego de Nicuesa, both young, both ambitious, both noblemen. To both he granted a ten-year right, naming Nicuesa governor of the western half, and Ojeda governor of the eastern. A line running through the Gulf of Urabá, into which the Atrato River emptied, was the boundary separating their territories.

Ojeda had once delighted Queen Isabella with his cool daring. He had, an eyewitness related, "walked out on a plank which jutted twenty feet out of the tower of the Cathedral of Seville, from where the men below seemed like dwarfs. Measuring it quickly with his feet, at the outside end of the plank he put one foot into the void and wheeled sharply around on the other, and then, with the same lightning speed and sureness, returned to the tower." His solo on the plank had made him an instant favorite.

Nicuesa had other gifts. He had served as carver to King Ferdinand's uncle, delighting the diners with his elegant dexterity; he charmed the court with his lute playing and thrilled them with his

exciting displays of horsemanship. As a courtier, his only shortcoming was his size, but he made up for his small stature by his extraordinary strength.

Both leaders had all the virtues and opportunities of wellborn, well-connected Spaniards. They were fierce fighters yet graceful courtiers, avid for personal glory yet utterly committed to their sovereign, savage against the infidels yet meek and docile to church and law. Pride governed their every act. They were too proud to be shrewd, to be cautious, to take advice, to consider ordinary men. For this pride both would pay with their lives.

Nicuesa, who had made a fortune in Hispaniola capturing Indians and selling them as slaves, could afford to make his expedition impressive. He equipped and supplied over seven hundred fighting men and colonists and purchased a fleet of ships to transport them. Ojeda who could keep his balance in the air could not make money on the ground. He smarted with shame when he saw, on arriving at Santo Domingo, how shabby and small his expedition was compared with Nicuesa's. His pride demanded that he match the size of his rival's expedition. With this in mind, Ojeda persuaded a successful lawyer, Martín Fernandez de Enciso, to invest in his expedition. Enciso was to follow Ojeda

as soon as he had collected men and supplies—
perhaps a matter of two months. In return for
furnishing additional men and supplies, Enciso was
offered a share of Ojeda's profits. The lawyer's last
waverings were overcome when Ojeda promised
him the position of mayor of the settlement which
Ojeda's grant required him to establish.

The eyes of Santo Domingo were on these three
—the high-spirited Ojeda, the arrogant Nicuesa,
and the shrewd, sharp Enciso. Especially were they
watched by Don Diego, Columbus's son, the governor of Hispaniola, who disliked both men for having ignored him when they secured their grants
from the king. At every turn he threw legal ob-
stacles in the way of Ojeda and Nicuesa. With the
town's eyes and ears occupied with the doings and
sayings of these two, Balboa could watch and plan
for himself. As a debtor he could not enlist. Though
he was a law-abiding man and though he risked
rotting in jail as a runaway debtor, Balboa had decided that nothing could keep him from grasping
this opportunity for which he had waited so long.
Both Ojeda's expedition and Nicuesa's were too
closely watched by the authorities for him to try
sneaking aboard. Balboa's only hope was Enciso's
party. Among the men hired by the lawyer were

some of Balboa's most trusted friends. The plan they made was simple, the timing carefully chosen. In the weeks that passed after Ojeda had finally given Don Diego's men the slip and sailed, and while Enciso was busy collecting everything he had agreed to furnish, Balboa and his friends did nothing that might attract attention or suspicion.

At last the time to put the plan into operation came.

In the tropics there is hardly a pause between the day's end and the oncoming night: a brief quarter of an hour of gloom before the lights spring to life in the darkness. On the final day when the cargo was being stowed away and the deck was crowded with last-minute supplies still arriving—when turmoil, confusion, and noise wrapped ship and shore in disordered activity, when Enciso's busy eyes could not check everything or watch everyone, when, in the quick twilight, movement was still sure-footed yet concealment possible—then they carried Balboa aboard. He must have made a bulky roll wrapped inside a sail, with his sword on one side and his dog close and quiet on the other. Yet nobody questioned the men staggering under the heavy canvas nor investigated the thick roll dumped in a dark corner of the hold.

They were well out to sea before he came out.

Circled by the men, Balboa and Enciso stood face to face. Somehow, as they took each other's measure, the advantage seemed to be with the stowaway, who by his bearing plainly showed he asked no favors but, instead, promised to prove his worth. He answered the questions put to him, giving his name and the town where he was born. He mentioned that he came of a good family and had been reared in a gentle manner. He would have said no more, but his friends prodded him to talk about the Pearl Coast to which they were sailing and which none of them had seen. Ah, yes! He remembered it well, very well—and he whetted Enciso's greed by talking familiarly of where Don Rodrigo had found pearls and the number of huge baskets heaped with treasure. He knew, he said, the weight of those baskets, for he had helped to carry the treasure overland to Santo Domingo when Bastidas's ship, made worthless by the *broma,* was lucky enough to reach the nearest point on Hispaniola before sinking. The mention of good luck and a harvest of pearls sounded sweet to Enciso.

As he spoke, Balboa watched the face of the man

who owned the vessel and all it held. He realized how much Enciso had to lose if anything went wrong. He wondered if the lawyer's possessions were what gave him his importance and speculated on what kind of man he would prove to be if, like Balboa, adversity stripped him of everything. He would not even have a dog as friend—and he patted Leoncico's head as the thought crossed his mind. Neither man gave offense nor spoke more than was necessary. Balboa did not seek to buy his way by revealing his secret; this he would do when the moment was right. Enciso did not humiliate or threaten this runaway debtor; this he would do when he was the mayor and could punish. For the present both were content that after many delays they were on their way at last and had a favoring wind and calm seas speeding them to the Pearl Coast. The future would declare itself. Enciso felt as the men watched and listened that they had welcomed Balboa—a fact that could be either good or ominous.

The boat ran before the wind, carrying them to the Gulf of Urabá, the rendezvous where they were to meet Ojeda.

III

The Fate of Ojeda and Nicuesa

Ojeda was the first to start for the Pearl Coast. He had been there before, in 1499—even before Bastidas—and though he had found no riches, he had won the support and friendship of Juan de la Cosa, his pilot, who had accompanied Columbus to America in 1492. On this present voyage Ojeda's three hundred men thought themselves very fortunate to have so experienced a leader and to have Cosa as captain-general of the four ships. Ojeda remembered the beautiful gulf he had traced on his previous voyage. It had been named "Little Venice" or Venezuela because the Indian houses lifted on stilts above a lagoon and the canoes they used in their comings and goings reminded him of Venice and her gondolas. But he would not return there. This time he thought of landing at the harbor they knew as Cartagena. Cosa warned him against that good harbor: The Indians who lived around its shores had made it deadly.

"Respect their arrows," Cosa warned Ojeda. "Be brave, but do not be foolhardy in reckoning with their slender reed arrows, for the tips dipped in a sly poison are deadly."

To Ojeda the words were not a warning; they were a challenge. No naked infidel was going to prevent him from landing wherever he pleased. His ships put in at Cartagena, a magnificent harbor hedged around by a thick forest. A large landing party, led by Ojeda and Cosa, went ashore. At first all went well. The Indians fell back before the Spaniards. Deeper and deeper into the forest the Indians retreated, the Spaniards following. And so they came to a large village which, after a brief, fierce fight, they won. Jubilant, the Spaniards scattered to search the houses for gold. Without warning the village was ringed by the blood-curdling war cries of the returning Indian warriors, who attacked, picking off the Spaniards with their poison-tipped arrows. What good were their stout Toledo swords when the merest scratch of an arrow brought quick paralysis and certain death? The poisoned arrows rained down on them. It was a massacre. Of the men who had marched ashore only Ojeda and one other survived. Among the dead, his body already black and bloated, was Juan de la Cosa. With him perished the knowledge of where along the Pearl Coast lived natives who did not tip their arrows with poison. His death left Balboa the only man in both expeditions who knew this all-important information.

This was the beginning of the long, slow, terrible destruction of Ojeda's pride. There was nothing he could say to the men waiting aboard the ships, nothing but that he lived and all the others lay dead, bristling with arrows. At that moment of agony Nicuesa's fleet, as splendid as it had been in the harbor of Santo Domingo, sailed into Cartagena. Nicuesa, forgetting his rivalry, shared Ojeda's desire for revenge. Together, at the head of four hundred men, they took the path back to the village. When night fell they attacked, killing the men, women, and children who lay asleep after

their earlier victory. Back safely at the harbor, the two leaders parted, each to take his own road to defeat and death.

Too late, Ojeda took Cosa's advice. But without Cosa to show him, he did not go far enough westward. The site he chose for his village was still within the area where the Indians poisoned their arrows. He named the stockaded village San Sebastián, invoking the help of the saint who had been pierced to death by arrows. The Indians, hidden and watchful, let the Spaniards land, fell trees, build houses, and surround them with a high, strong stockade. All this they permitted without interference, knowing all the time that the hated intruders were building their own cage, a cage in which they would be penned by poisoned arrows. Indeed the Spaniards soon realized that only within the stout walls of San Sebastián were they safe from sudden death. Closely confined within their settlement, they first knew hunger and then death from starvation. Of the three hundred vigorous, eager men who had asked to join the expedition, only sixty men still lived when unexpectedly a ship manned by treasure-hunting desperadoes appeared.

Ojeda took this unlikely opportunity to return to Hispaniola and seek help. He promised those he left behind at San Sebastián that even if he did not live to reach Santo Domingo they could expect Enciso and his two ships to arrive momentarily with supplies.

Ojeda was fated never to see Enciso again. He managed to return to Santo Domingo alive, his pride shattered, his body sick, his pockets empty. There, soon after, he died.

It was not at San Sebastián that the survivors of Ojeda's party met Enciso. Near Cartagena thirty-five men crowded into a brigantine hailed his two ships. Enciso could hardly believe what he saw: emaciated, exhausted men led by a common soldier named Francisco Pizarro. Thus the future conqueror of Peru made his appearance in history. Enciso flatly refused to believe Pizarro's story that Ojeda had entrusted the command to him. As though he were a witness in a law court, Pizarro was asked where Ojeda was. Ojeda? Oh, weeks before he had left their settlement, San Sebastián, risking his life to seek help. And Pizarro even produced a document, signed by Ojeda and duly notarized, in which he named Pizarro his lieutenant and gave him permission to lead the men back to Hispaniola if Ojeda did not return within fifty days.

To the lawyer this story smelled of lies, the document of forgery. He suspected Pizarro's men had murdered Ojeda, because they offered him gold to be permitted to continue on to Hispaniola.

Enciso was not to be bribed. Already he was trembling for the safety of his investment. And when he caught sight of Balboa questioning Pizarro about San Sebastián's location, he was certain the two were conspiring. He commanded the survivors to return with him to San Sebastián where, as mayor, he would punish them for deserting. There, too, he would make certain that the stowaway, Balboa, would be dealt with as the law for runaway debtors prescribed.

Almost within sight of San Sebastián it was Enciso's turn to taste misfortune. He could blame no one when the larger of his ships grounded on a sandbar running across the mouth of the harbor. Minutes later the pounding waves had robbed him of most of his possessions—his cannon and weapons sank, the horses and swine penned up for the voyage drowned. The men, peeling off their clothes that they might swim, reached the shore almost naked. They managed to salvage a few barrels of flour and a dozen cheeses. Shaken by their sudden misfortune, they were swept by fear when, rounding the point of land back of which lay San Sebastián, they saw that the houses and stockade which the survivors had left a few days before were nothing but dead ashes and charred logs. In its desolation Enciso's party was imprisoned, for if anyone ventured out to hunt game or pick wild plums and cabbage palms a shower of arrows made him run back.

Where should they go? Was there no place free from an enemy who could not be seen and whose poisoned arrows made him invincible? How could they all escape in the two boats left? When misery and despair gripped all, including Enciso, Balboa stood up so everyone could hear him. For this moment of crisis he had waited. For this he had cherished his secret all these years.

"I remember," he said, "that in past years we came along this coast with Don Rodrigo to explore. I remember that we came to a gulf and disembarked on its western shore. There we found a town seated amid abundant, fertile fields and inhabited by people who did not dip their arrows in poison." He

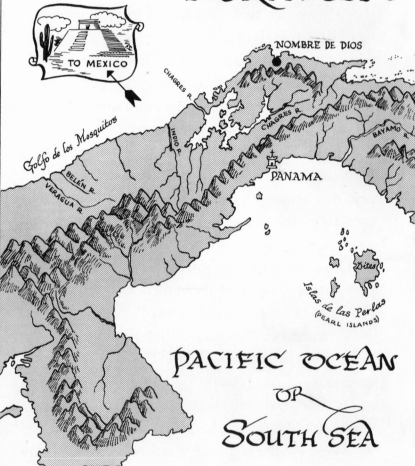

ISTHMUS OF
PANAMA

CARIBBEAN
OR NORTH SEA

NOMBRE DE DIOS

TO MEXICO

CHAGRES R.

CHAGRES R.

INDIO R.

Golfo de los Mosquitos

BAYAMO R.

PANAMA

BELÉN R.

VERAGUA R.

Dites

Islas de las Perlas
(PEARL ISLANDS)

PACIFIC OCEAN
OR
SOUTH SEA

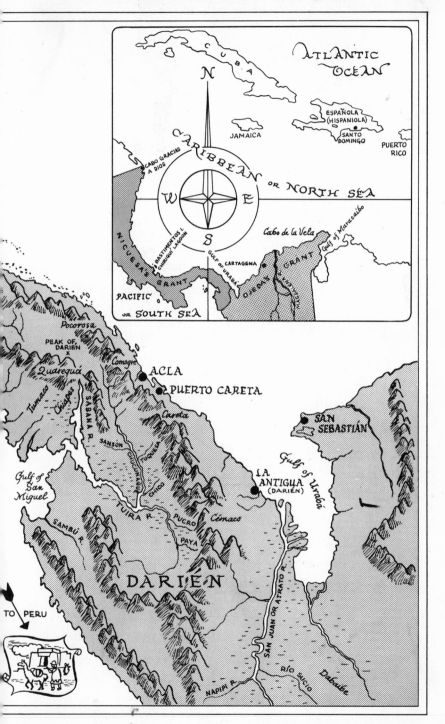

ATLANTIC OCEAN

CUBA

JAMAICA

ESPAÑOLA (HISPANIOLA)

SANTO DOMINGO

PUERTO RICO

CARIBBEAN or NORTH SEA

N

W E

S

CABO GRACIAS A DIOS

BASTIMENTOS I.
CHIRIQUI LAGOON

NICUESA'S GRANT

PACIFIC or SOUTH SEA

Cabo de la Vela

GULF of CARTAGENA

Gulf of Maracaibo

Gulf of Urabá

OJEDA'S GRANT

MAGDALENA R.

Pocorosa

PEAK OF DARIEN ×

Quarequá

Tumaco

Chiapes

Comogre

ACLA

PUERTO CARETA

Careta

SAN SEBASTIÁN

Gulf of San Miguel

SABANA R.

SANSON

CHUCUNAQUÉ

TUQUESA

CHICO

TUIRA R.

PUCRO

PAYA

Cémaco

LA ANTIGUA (DARIÉN)

Gulf of Urabá

SAMBÚ R.

DARIÉN

TO PERU

SAN JUAN OR ATRATO R.

NAPIPI R.

RÍO SUCIO

Dabaibe

went on to tell them how wide and deep the Gulf of Urabá was and how different from one another were the people who dwelt on its shores. "Just as the lands of the man-eating Indians are poor and unproductive, so rich are the villages on the other side. There Indians have gardens to feed us, cotton cloth with which we can cover our nakedness, and golden ornaments finely wrought."

His words, authoritative and assured, filled them with hope. Balboa restored their courage by offering to take them to a region where they could survive, and he had a plan whereby a small party of tough fighters would cross over to the western shore of the Gulf of Urabá. There they would conquer the people of Darién, as that land was called.

In two brigantines they sailed to the village. When Cémaco, the chief of the Darién Indians, saw the Spaniards approaching, he ordered the women and children to hide in the forest while he and his five hundred warriors prepared for battle. The naked Indians, armed only with wooden swords, were no match for the steel and gunpowder of the Spaniards, and after a brief and bloody fight, Cémaco and his surviving men fled to the forest. Not a Spaniard had been lost, and Enciso led his soldiers

into the village to take possession. In the huts of
the Indians they found the treasure they had been
seeking: shining plates and anklets and bracelets of
beaten gold.

The rest of the Spaniards were soon ferried over.
Santa María de la Antigua del Darién was the name
the 180 men gave their town; it was to be the first
successful settlement established on the mainland
of the New World.

But what of Nicuesa, the gay and gifted courtier
whom the king had honored with a royal grant?
What of Nicuesa whose fine fleet and 785 men were
sailing toward their territory on the western end
of Panama? His story is brief and bitter. His ships
were caught on shoals and there destroyed; the
men found themselves on a desolate coast plagued
by clouds of mosquitoes. Nicuesa was bewildered.
He did not know where on that marshy shore his
domain began. He ordered his men eastward, and so
they walked along the Caribbean shore, dragging
a small boat, a sorry remainder of their proud fleet.

They walked for days and weeks. Men died of
hunger and fever. Only sixty-five were left when
at last they came to a village surrounded by gardens.
"In the Name of God, let us stop here," Nicuesa

cried out when he saw this welcome oasis that offered them food and rest. In the Name of God— Nombre de Dios—was what they called this lone settlement in an empty land. The Indians had timidly abandoned it at the approach of the Spaniards. Nicuesa's men had no one to threaten them, but neither did they have the chance to survive without natives to teach them how to live in the New World.

Not long after they had occupied the village, a ship appeared and made straight for the colony. The brigantine was one of those commanded by Colmenares, whom Nicuesa had entrusted to bring out additional settlers and supplies. He had landed them, he said, within Nicuesa's territory at a Spanish colony whose inhabitants called it Santa María de la Antigua del Darién. Then, fearing that disaster had overtaken his commander, Colmenares had come searching for Nicuesa. Two men from the community had loyally joined Colmenares in the search. Now they invited Nicuesa, their lawful governor, to the settlement. Proudly they described Darién as a miracle of safety and plenty, of good gardens and gold. It was, they knew, his domain and to it they bid him welcome.

Then they heard Nicuesa reply. His first act as governor—his manner was haughty, his voice rasping as he answered them—would be to confiscate all the gold they had collected and punish those who had dared to trespass on his monopoly.

Had Nicuesa's privations driven him mad? Could he be as callous and greedy as he sounded? Whatever doubts the envoys had were answered when some of Nicuesa's men showed, near Nombre de Dios, a grim area called the Dying Place to which the pitiless leader sent men too weak to work. There at the Dying Place, as a scapegoat for his misfortunes, Nicuesa had taken revenge on his luckless pilot-general by keeping him tied to a stake.

Acting with great caution the two emissaries from Darién paid Nicuesa a respectful farewell, asking leave to go on ahead to prepare a proper reception for him. Then they hurried back to their village to warn their fellow settlers and describe the kind of man their governor had become.

When, a few days later, Nicuesa, aboard the ship Colmenares had brought him, approached the shore at Darién, Balboa, Enciso, Pizarro, and all the colonists stood on the beach awaiting him. But it was not in welcome. Across the intervening waters he heard the town crier: "Stop! Do not try to land. Return to Nombre de Dios." And then the notary read a resolution he had witnessed: "In the sight of God and the King: The Town officers and all the townsmen of Santa María de la Antigua del Darién have taken solemn oath not to accept Don Diego de Nicuesa as their lawful governor. It is further voted that any of the party of Don Diego who choose to stay at Santa María de la Antigua del Darién are hereby invited; and whosoever of the colonists desire to leave and accompany Don Diego are free to do so." The voice was firm, the words clearly heard. With the colonists' decision there was no arguing, no compromise. Without setting foot on shore, Nicuesa returned to his ship; seventeen men went with him. Where and how they perished we do not know.

Now neither of the two leaders who had started off to the flourish of royal favor remained. Martín de Enciso stood with the men of Darién on the beach that fateful day, a colonist like the others, neither richer nor more important. In the short space of time between the capture of Darién and the appearance of Nicuesa he had held authority and lost it. Because he had paid Ojeda to be mayor of his settlement, he had immediately assumed the office he believed to be rightfully his and had sought to regulate the trading the men had started—selling back to the Indians their own captured utensils of wood and clay and their cotton coverlets for gold. His restrictions had made every man his enemy. They, in turn, had accused Enciso of seizing office illegally. "Where is your contract from Ojeda?" they taunted him maliciously, knowing he had come ashore as naked as any of them. They quickly deposed him and threatened to put him on trial. Then, because all the colonists wanted their settlement to have a proper government and to protect themselves from misrule, they elected two mayors, Balboa and Martín de Zamudio, a quiet, honorable man. These two, as duly elected officials, had flanked the town crier when he bade Nicuesa leave.

Such divided authority gave Enciso an opportunity to keep some power by creating factions and distrust. Balboa knew that a colony broken into cliques and hostile groups would not survive. To prevent this he suggested that it was the colonists' most immediate duty to report the establishment of Darién and the state of its affairs to the governor of Hispaniola, Don Diego Colón, and to King Fer-

dinand. The colonists approved of Balboa's proposal
to send the lawyer Enciso and Balboa's co-mayor,
Zamudio. They would carry gifts to impress the
governor and the king with Darién's rich promise
of wealth. And they also sent an elderly colonist,
Juan de Valdivia, to secure from Hispaniola the
help of additional colonists and much-needed supplies.

By this move Balboa thought to free himself
from both rivals. By having them leave together he
hoped each would act as watchdog over the other.
In the time he would be alone he would have the
opportunity to prove by great deeds accomplished
and great treasure accumulated that he, Vasco
Nuñez de Balboa, was the man whom the king
should recognize as head of Santa María de la Antigua del Darién.

The month was April, the year 1511, when the
envoys sailed in one of the brigantines Colmenares
had brought. Balboa remained undisputed leader of
the colony.

IV

An Interruption:
A Word About America

It takes an effort to remember and, remembering, to imagine what confusion there was about the size and shape and position of the New World when Balboa began his discoveries in 1511. Seventeen years earlier, when Columbus first set sail from Spain in the *Santa María,* everyone believed that nothing but a single ocean lay between him and the Orient. When he returned to Spain in 1493, Columbus spoke of the islands he had discovered as "the Indies." During his next three voyages, and up until his death in 1506, he continued to insist that

"the Indies" were savage islands in the Indian
Ocean.

But in 1501 Amerigo Vespucci, an Italian skilled
in mathematics and astronomy, sailed in the service
of Portugal to explore the extent and shape of the
lands south of the Equator. He often went ashore
on the South American coast in order to use the
proper scientific methods for determining longitude. Vespucci's figures showed that the distance
from Spain to China must be far greater than
Columbus had declared it to be. His figures also
led him to declare that the coasts he had explored
bordered a new continent, nowhere connected with
Asia. A new world!

Vespucci's Latin letters describing his exciting
new ideas were widely read in Europe. A mapmaker
named Martin Waldseemüller reprinted them in
his book, *Cosmographiae Introductio,* which appeared in 1507. His book not only contained Vespucci's letters but also explained Waldseemüller's
revolutionary new map, based on Vespucci's find-
ings, which showed a huge island continent—
labeled "America"—lying between Europe and
Asia. "I do not see why we should rightly refuse to
name it America," wrote Waldseemüller, "after

its discoverer Americus, a man of sagacious mind."
And beyond this newly named America, mapmaker
Waldseemüller boldly placed an ocean whose eastern shore no European had ever seen; an ocean
whose vastness no European ship had ever sailed.
For this was the Pacific, which Balboa had yet to
discover, and which Magellan had yet to cross.

Vespucci's remarkable letters and Waldseemüller's map were eagerly studied by Europe's
learned geographers and rulers. But it is important
to understand that in 1511 most Spaniards were
primarily interested in possessing themselves of
these strange lands. Arguments as to whether Columbus had discovered "the Indies" he had first
reported or instead a vast new world had little
meaning for the adventurous Spaniards on Hispaniola. It is hardly possible that Balboa ever saw
Waldseemüller's map.

When Balboa began his explorations in Darién,
navigators were voyaging along the Atlantic coast
of the Americas, busily probing the rivers and bays
for a passageway to the Orient, trying to understand the secrets of its long shoreline. None had investigated the land that lay beyond.

The story of Balboa is the story of his search:

how he found out where to go, what to look for, and how to deal with the unexpected events that followed from his discovery. The first European to explore the American mainland, he opened a door into the unknown. He was a man whose desire to learn was stronger than his fears, a leader whose personal qualities met every test. He was eager to find out anything and everything he could about this new land. He knew that just as he had saved an expedition, apparently doomed, by having learned where, exactly where, the Indians did not poison their arrows, so he would win wealth, fame, and power by exploring the land.

When Balboa plunged into the Darién wilderness, he had no maps of the interior to guide him. He could not even be positively sure that Darién was not just another island, like Hispaniola. There was no way for him to know that he had brought his men to the eastern end of that narrow, arched land-bridge that connects the continents of North and South America: the Isthmus of Panama. It would take him many painful months of exploration to learn what each of us knows: that the Isthmus lies on an east-west line, separating the Caribbean Sea on its northern coast from the Pacific Ocean on the south.

Yet soon Balboa and his men began to suspect that they were on no puny island. Even this narrowest part of the New World had continental proportions. The easiest route into the densely wooded interior was up the Darién river which the Indians called the Atrato. Balboa's party sloshed through a stream too shallow for boats and too dangerous for canoes, for its pools held uprooted trees whose branches were mired in mud. The river led to a swamp. Beyond was the forest, a mighty thicket of giants whose high, leafy tops were laced together by vines to make an umbrella that shaded the forest floor. The sun, so hot and glaring, never reached the ground inside the forest; there a twilight gloom blotted out the directions of the sun's rising and setting. It was a place to get lost in and perish. Balboa knew that without a guide he dare not risk exploring it.

As far as he could see, the forest covered the land except where rivers and swamps cut paths and made openings; it even concealed the presence of the mountain range that runs the length of the

Isthmus and separates its two coasts. The forests and swamps would have to wait until he had guides and until he knew what to look for.

Months later, after he had found Indian guides, he wrote a letter to King Ferdinand and used understatement to describe the terrible size of the swamps. "The swamps of this land are not such light affairs that we move through them joyfully. Many times we have to go naked through marshes and water for one and two leagues with our clothing collected and placed on the shield on top of the head. And leaving some marshes, we enter into others and proceed in this manner two and three and ten days."

The food of the New World Indians fascinated the Spaniards. Strange cereals and plants grew in their well-tended gardens. There was a knobby root the Indians called potatoes. Columbus had presented a few to Their Majesties Ferdinand and Isabella, who considered them a great delicacy and ate them as a preserve, or a relish, spiced and steeped in wine. The common Spaniards mistook them for turnips or firm mushrooms and nibbled them raw until the Indians taught them how tasty and satisfying they were when roasted in the fire. Here the Spaniards first experimented with other plants related to the potato: the tomato grown for its red fruit, and tobacco grown for its leaves—Europe was certain that men who blew out smoke were devils, not humans.

Wheat, rye, oats—none of the European grains which could be sown broadcast and grown in bulk were found in the New World. Whatever else an Indian raised, his garden always had corn, beans, and squash, crops that required intense work—first with a pointed planting stick and later with a hoe. The Spaniards noticed that these three were planted together, each trio in a separate hillock that they might furnish one another with support and shade. Their only cereal, the great Indian staple, was corn, which they called maize. Because the Indians were so dependent on their maize, beans, and squash, they were planted with special ceremonies and harvested with thanksgiving festivals. The Spaniards also marveled at the way the Darién Indians used whatever was edible. Their flat bread, for example, had a kind of magic in its preparation. From the shredded roots of the cassava plant they washed out a deadly, poisonous juice and used the pulp to make a flour that was safe and wholesome.

Even more noticeable were the differences between the animals of Europe and those of the New
World. The Indians had no horses, no donkeys, no
oxen—none of the animals that pull the plow and
carry loads. As a consequence they had no wagons,
and the wheel, which throughout the Old World
also served to mass-produce pottery and harness
the power of wind and water, was used only as
part of an Indian toy, attached to a little cart that
children pulled about. Nor did the Indians have
barnyard animals—cattle, sheep, goats, and pigs—
to provide them with meat, milk and cheese, wool
and leather; and except for the turkey, they raised
no farm fowl—no chickens, ducks, or geese. Lack-
ing such animals, the Indians hunted and fished to
augment the maize, beans, and squash they raised.

It should be said that the Spaniards in Darién
never saw the American buffalo. "Nothing to see
but cattle and sky" was how Coronado, the first
European to lead an expedition to the edge of the
Great Plains, described that vast grassland. Not
until fifty years after Columbus did the Spaniards
come to know the mighty American buffalo, magnificent in size and mighty in number. Another two
hundred years would pass before the horse would

run wild on the plains. Mustangs and Indian ponies —swift and sturdy, smart and proud—arrived there when Spanish settlers moving northward from Mexico into the upper Rio Grande valley brought with them oxen, mules, and goats, flocks of sheep, and hundreds of horses. Soon the Indians of the plains appreciated how the horse would revolutionize their way of life. For of all the animals the Europeans introduced, it was only the horse they made part of their world. As J. Frank Dobie, the great historian of the plains, says, "It made them masters of the illimitable herds of buffalo that gave them food, shelter, bedding, raiment, tools, saddles, lariats, twine, and the core of their religion."

V

How Balboa Found
the First Clue

Soon after Enciso and Zamudio had sailed, Balboa started sending out small parties to search for food; keeping the men fed and fit was Balboa's main concern. Mindful of the dreadful conditions at Nombre de Dios, he order Colmenares—who had chosen to live with the colonists rather than die with the foolish, arrogant Nicuesa—to take two brigantines and bring back any survivors of Nicuesa's group who were stranded there. On the homeward voyage from that rescue mission, Colmenares sighted two figures who signaled the ships. Sailing close to the shore, they saw two men as naked and painted as Indians, who called to them in Spanish. Some of Nicuesa's former colonists at Nombre de Dios recognized them as comrades who had fled from the main party when Nicuesa ordered them punished unjustly. It was a meeting unexpected and wonderful. The two painted men related how, when they were almost dead, they had been found by Indians whose chief, Careta, had permitted them to live in his village. And then, without a thought of gratitude to the Indians, the two told how well supplied with food the village was and how simple it would be for the Spaniards to get it. They perfected the plan for betraying Careta: One of them was to accompany Colmenares to Darién so that he could later act as a guide; the other was to return to the village to avoid any suspicion.

As soon as they came to Darién, Balboa heard the guide's story. Immediately he knew that this was the opportunity he had needed. He acted quickly and coolly. Picking 130 of his toughest, strongest men to accompany him overland, Balboa pushed on as fast as he could. He and his men had about a hundred miles to go. At the same time he ordered the two ships to follow him up the coast. He was so certain of success that he wanted to have them with him to bring back the food and treasure he expected to capture.

Careta, at the head of his two thousand warriors, came out to meet Balboa. With the resident Spaniard acting as interpreter, he conversed with the new chief of Darién. He invited the Spaniards into his village and offered them food and drink. First, Balboa tried asking for provisions. Careta was sorry that he had none to spare. Both men were polite, both were friendly, and after a pleasant exchange of words, Balboa said good-bye and left. He decided to take by trickery what Careta had refused to give him. The Spaniards had not gone far when night fell and hid their movements. Turning around, they came back to the sleeping village. Without having to fire their guns they captured the chief and his family, and then, guided by the two spies, they helped themselves to the village's great supplies of food. When morning came the captives and food were loaded on the brigantines bound for Darién.

During the voyage Careta had time to recover from the shock of the ambush and the humiliation of being a captive; he also had time to think over how expertly the ruse had been carried out. It would be better, he decided, to be the friend and

ally of so capable a leader than to spend his life as a
captive or an enemy.

"Set me, my family, and people free," he said to
Balboa, "and we will remain your friends. We will
take care of your fields and supply you with food.
We will show you the riches of the land." And then,
as a pledge of his good faith, he brought his daughter and placed her hand in Balboa's. "Here is my
daughter. Take her for your wife. Her life will
guarantee our faithful friendship."

Balboa accepted. He needed an Indian of importance and intelligence as a friend much more
than he needed captives. Here was the friend who
could guide him safely through the jungle forest
and also through the tangle of tribal alliances so
that he, Balboa, could win the goals he desired. And
so Careta, from having been Balboa's captive, became his father-in-law. Neither was ever to regret
the pact they made. When they reached Darién the
alliance was suitably celebrated and Careta remained as a respected guest for three days. Balboa
showed him wonders never before seen in the New
World. Spanish horses were bridled and saddled
and put through their paces for him; he had guns
shot off in his honor and a concert given for his

pleasure. When Careta left he received gifts of greater value than the food the Spaniards had taken from him—knives, axes, and needles of precious steel. Also, Balboa promised that he would help him fight his enemies.

The Spaniards lost no time in keeping this promise. The first to feel the force of this new alliance was Ponca, an ancient foe of Careta's, who fled to the forest at Balboa's approach. After the Spaniards had stripped Ponca's village of everything they wanted, they set it afire to punish him. More than ever Careta was impressed with his son-in-law and suggested that it would be useful if he made a treaty with Comogre, a chief who ruled a rich, important territory to the west and who could put three thousand warriors into battle. At the same time he sent messengers to Comogre, urging him to make friends with Darién's strong new ruler. Comogre agreed to receive Balboa in peace.

After all the thatched-roofed houses they had seen, the Spaniards were impressed by the size and splendor of Comogre's palace. The building was 150 paces long and 80 paces wide and surrounded by a stone wall that set it apart from the village. Great beams rose from a floor smooth and polished

to support a carved ceiling. Within the palace they were shown spacious living apartments and huge storerooms filled with maize, cassava bread, dried fruits and meats, and garden produce. At last, in Comogre's own living quarters, they came to an innermost sanctuary where they saw a weird sight. Here were mummies, Comogre's ancestors, the supernatural guard of the tribe's power and prosperity, whose bodies had been carefully preserved by a long drying process over a slow fire. Dressed in cotton robes, they hung from the ceiling arranged according to their rank. Masks of pure beaten gold encrusted with pearls and precious stones covered their faces.

As evidence of his wealth and as a token of his friendship, Comogre presented Balboa with many slaves captured in a raid and four thousand ounces of beautifully wrought gold. At the sight of this glittering pile of golden objects, the Spaniards, always prepared and always obedient to their king's commands, brought out scales and smelting tools so that they could set aside the royal fifth—the Crown took twenty percent of all treasure. Then they began to divide the rest, as they had agreed, among themselves. As they weighed and counted

and distributed, every Spaniard paid close attention. At times they disagreed and argued. Then they
grew angry and began shouting. Comogre's eldest
son suddenly knocked over the scales, scattering the
gold all over the room.

"How badly you behave, O Christians!" he addressed the thunderstruck Spaniards. "Is your
thirst for gold so great that to quench it you attack
peaceful people and exile yourselves from your
homeland to search for it? You destroy the beauty
of these necklaces when you melt them into ingots;
yet we have no more value for such unworked gold
than we would have for a lump of clay before it
has been made into a vase that pleases our taste or
serves our need. If it is just the crude, raw gold you
crave, I will show you a region where it is to be
found and where you can collect enough to satisfy
the thirst that torments you."

Silent, the Spaniards looked at this naked youth
who spoke so passionately and who regarded them
with haughty scorn while the interpreter was trans-
lating his words. He pointed to the mountain range
and said: "Quarequá rules the pass over the mountains. If you can capture his town, you will see from
the other side another sea on which your little boats

have never sailed but which is navigated by people who, though they are as naked as we, use both sails and oars. On the other side of the mountains all the streams are very rich in gold. King Tubanamá is ruler of the richest kingdom—why, his kitchen utensils and garden tools are made of gold, since gold is to him as iron is to you! He will use all his strength to stop you. Because you are our friend, you are his enemy." He stopped, for the Spaniards were talking and laughing among themselves. The interpreter told him they thought he was joking when he spoke of pots and pans made of gold, that a man would be crazy to believe such wild words.

"Listen to me, Christians." Comogre's son knew he had to convince these eager but doubting men. He spoke loudly, as if that would make them understand. "I will prove the truth of what I say. I will stop your suspicions. I myself will go as your guide and you may hang me from the first tree if you do not find that I have told you the exact truth. If you can overthrow Quarequá and destroy King Tubanamá you will shatter the power of our enemies and free us from the fear of attack, the fear under which we, like our ancestors, live. This will be our reward for guiding you and helping you, for

my father's warriors will fight by your side. And
you, O Christians, you will get all the gold you have
thirsted for.

"Summon, I urge you, summon a thousand well-
armed soldiers. Together we will break the power
of King Tubanamá. We shall have our peace and
you your gold."

Not one of the Spaniards doubted the truth of
the words so passionately spoken. To Balboa the
words were the door which opened onto everything
he wanted—gold, gold and the renown which
would come with the discovery of an unknown sea.
Their promise dazzled him. His gratitude to Comogre and especially to his brave son made him
want to share with them and all their people his
most precious possession: He would make them
Christians. Balboa himself stood as godfather to the
young man, naming the chief's son Carlos in honor
of the prince who would soon rule Spain.

Now he must return to Darién to get everything
ready. He must be certain of success when he attempted to kick open the door guarded by Quarequá and gather the treasure of Tubanamá.

VI
What Happened at Darién

When had men ever had such news as was brought back by Balboa's party? Within grasp, and theirs for the mere taking, was a treasure that since the Day of Creation had been waiting for the Spaniards. So great an expectation made men tremble when they dared think of it.

Before he could allow himself to think of it, Balboa had to solve serious immediate problems; before they could cross the mountains to collect the gold, the settlers had to have an assured food supply and security from attack. As head of the colony, Balboa could not run the risk of returning to find Darién either a starvation camp or an empty, charred ruin: Darién must not repeat the bitter experience of either Nombre de Dios or San Sebastián. He knew how narrow was the margin separating the colony from disaster. More and more, parties going beyond the settlement were being ambushed and attacked by Cémaco, the Darién chief, who, from the forest to which he and his warriors had fled, watched and waited for opportunities to hit back.

For himself, for his own peace of spirit, Balboa needed to be certain of his position. True, the men had elected him their leader, but he wanted that position confirmed by a decree from the governor of Hispaniola, Don Diego Colón, or better still—best of all—by the king himself. Until his authority was officially approved he remained at the mercy of every malicious whisper and intrigue, of every peevish complaint and fickle mood.

At last help came from Hispaniola. All Darién turned out to welcome Valdivia, who had accompanied Enciso and Zamudio as far as Hispaniola almost six months before. His small boat was loaded with as much food as it could safely carry and he brought the promise of further supplies to be sent regularly. Don Diego had been generous because he knew how precarious life was for the Darién colonists, who had to live like the Indians. Despite the admirable fertility of the land of the New World— Europeans marveled at how fast and large the plants grew—sudden storms robbed the gardens of their promise and abundance. Old residents had seen how often fields of maize that stood almost ready for the picking had been flattened by hurricanes or had watched when cloudbursts washed out the ripe plenty of gardens. Hispaniola had suffered from this same feast-or-famine gamble until livestock and supplies imported from Spain provided food reserves and protected the settlers against the loss of their crops.

Valdivia delivered Don Diego's letter notifying Balboa of his appointment as temporary mayor of Darién and related that in conversations Don Diego had shown his anger at the large number of lives needlessly and foolishly wasted by Ojeda and Nicuesa. What Valdivia did not know—what he could not know for the news arrived after he had left Hispaniola—was that the king had written approving Don Diego's recognition of Balboa as temporary mayor.

Soon the supplies Valdivia had brought were exhausted and the men were back on half rations; again their food reserves were insufficient and uncertain. Again Valdivia was told to sail to Hispaniola to ask for more supplies. To sweeten the request and to thank him for the honor shown him, Balboa wrote to Don Diego. Proudly, in great detail, he related what he had done and what he had learned —the wonderful and joyous news of the South Sea given by Comogre's son, Carlos. Balboa also wrote a letter to be forwarded to the king. With it went the fifth reserved for the Crown, two hundred pounds of gold. In addition, for Don Diego as well as for the king, he added a few heavy gold ingots from his own share. Many of the men entrusted their shares of the golden spoils to Valdivia to be forwarded to their families or creditors in Spain. The small caravel carrying much of Darién's treasure and all of her hopes left that January: 1512 had begun.

Let us stop for a moment to tell the fate of this ship and its singular sequel.

Valdivia and the ship with its treasure and hopes, its dazzling announcement of a new sea and its sober request for aid, never arrived in Hispaniola.

Seven years later, in 1519, when Cortés was planning the conquest of Mexico, he knew how invaluable an interpreter would be and set about finding one from among the Spaniards known to be held captive by Indian tribes in Yucatán. Through natives who traded between the mainland and the islands, he sent letters out to the unknown captives as well as trinkets for them to use in ransoming themselves. One man, and only one, came to the island rendezvous in answer to Cortés's invitation. It was from him that the terrible fate of Valdivia's party became known.

"My name is Jerónimo de Aguilar," said the man who looked like an Indian although he spoke Spanish. "When I was sent to the New World I had already taken my vows as a friar: Chastity, poverty, and obedience. I sought to observe them while serving God among the Indians. How the Devil tried me is a long story and I would be brief. The caravel on which I was returning to Hispaniola was finally swallowed by the hungry seas, which for three days had been sending tongues of water over her as though to taste her quality. Eight of us reached the shore alive. Indians found us and brought us to their village. We were confined. But we were well treated and well fed. Very well fed, Señor Capitán. Thus some placid weeks passed. We were happy to be alive and not unhappy at our treatment. And then one dreadful, dreadful day four of us—they were the sturdiest—were led outside our pen. We watched them go and could see—they had not walked very far—how suddenly they were caught and slaughtered like pigs. God help them! They were spitted, roasted, and eaten.

"When we had recovered from our shock and the horror and anguish, we understood our fate. We were being saved for the next feast. We laid plans to escape from the cannibals. Two, another and myself, succeeded. We reached a distant tribe who did not practice this abominable habit. There we were again taken captive.

"There your letter found me serving my master in a position of trust. I hastened to my friend, for my master was willing that he, too, could leave. But he would not. Though I pleaded with him, he would not. Nor would he say why until I sought to stir his heart with talk of Spain. 'Brother Aguilar,' he said, shaking his head, 'I am married and have three children. The Indians look on me as a leader in

peace and a chieftain in war. My face is tattooed
and my ears pierced. How can I return to Spain?' "

Brother Aguilar, who had sailed from Darién in
1512, was to be at Cortés's side eight years later in
Mexico when they were admitted to the presence of
the Aztec emperor, the great Moctezuma. But this
was all in the future; let us return to the time when
Valdivia set sail for Hispaniola.

Until more supplies came from Don Diego, Balboa had the settlers to feed. As before he had to rely
on what foraging or raiding parties brought in. A
rumor led him to invade a certain swamp. The
rumor told of great quantities of gold kept in the
temple of a goddess sacred to a tribe whose territory
lay within the limits of the swamp. The Spaniards
found the tribe—an amazing people who had taken
to the treetops to be safe from floods and enemies.
From their high houses they pelted the Spaniards
with stones; and to make them submit, and in order
to search them for gold and food, the Spaniards had
to chop down the trees in which they nested. All
their hard work brought them no treasure and little
food.

Their raids had one serious result, however. They

increased the number of hostile tribes and finally united these tribes, usually warring with each other, into an alliance. The ever-watchful Cémaco, chief of the Darién Indians, used this common hatred of the Spaniards to cement five tribes into a pact and a plot. Each of the five chiefs was to mobilize one thousand fighting men and provide twenty canoes; for if five thousand warriors were to attack Darién in strength, their overwhelming numbers could wipe out the intruder who threatened them all. In their pact they agreed on the division of the Spaniards' possessions—guns, knives, nails, and pots— for the Indians desired iron as strongly as the Europeans hungered for gold. And to keep so large a number of warriors together and maintain them, great quantities of provisions were collected at Tichiri, Cémaco's new village, established some distance up the Atrato River.

Balboa first heard of this plot from one of his men, the sole survivor of a small group that had been ambushed while out on a foraging mission. The man knew only that an attack on the colony had been planned. That same night one of Balboa's Indian sweethearts repeated the same story and was able to tell him the location of the village where the attackers were encamped. That was the one fact Balboa needed to know.

Balboa struck and struck hard. With seventy tough, tried men he marched overland, approaching Tichiri from its unguarded rear while Colmenares, with an equal number of men, paddled up the Atrato. They met at Tichiri and, taking the enemy by surprise, smashed the Indian defense. Again Cémaco, the wily Darién chief, slipped away; but four of the chiefs were captured and hanged on the spot. Without the leaders who had held the separate tribes together, the Indians lost their unity. They were powerless. The moment when they could have wiped out the Spaniards had passed; now the panic-stricken people accepted peace on Balboa's terms. Hundreds of warriors washed off their war paint and meekly carried the great store of collected food from Tichiri to Darién.

At a single stroke Balboa had saved the settlement from attack and made himself master of provisions sufficient to carry Darién through its infancy.

It was his behavior in handling the plot that revealed Balboa's remarkable qualities of leadership. His prompt, vigorous action proved that he was

not frightened by an enemy of vastly superior
numbers, and by limiting his wrath to the execu-
tion of the responsible leaders—a quick and pointed
punishment whose meaning was clear to their followers—he tempered his dreadful act with mercy
and forgiveness. Such moderation in killing, rare
both in the Spanish and in the Indian worlds, dis-
solved the Indians' enmity into feelings of gratitude, esteem, and friendship.

Within the next few months Balboa showed that
he could also handle the skulduggery of Spanish
plotters. Petty intrigue was the price he paid for
the ease and peace Darién enjoyed in the months
following the great Indian plot. No longer were the
men prisoners of their hunger, no longer were they
fearful of traveling outside the settlement. With
Indian slaves to tend their gardens, they no longer
had to toil in the tropical heat. Malcontents now
had time to cultivate their spites and mean preten-
sions. Balboa had made Darién a prize to be grabbed
at by greedy, jealous men, and such were Corral, a
lawyer, and his friend Rua. Their accomplices were
those who had supported Enciso and Nicuesa. Their
method was to accuse Balboa of having been unfair
in the division of treasure.

Then Balboa showed his cunning. He did not try to defend himself. He knew that he had given each man a just and liberal share of the spoils—the gold and slaves. He would set a trap, baiting it with a quantity of gold hidden where the agitators would be sure to find it. Having done this, he announced he was going hunting—and left. When Corral and Rua heard that Balboa was to be gone for a while, they searched his quarters and found the gold. Claiming it theirs by right, they and their followers took it. But so greedy were the two leaders in what they kept for themselves and so stingy in what they distributed that their followers turned on them in disillusionment and anger. They held Corral and Rua prisoners, awaiting Balboa's return. After Corral and Rua's attempt, no one tried to threaten the firm bond of allegiance between the colonists and Balboa.

VII
What Happened in Spain

The year was passing and still no word had come
from Valdivia. Sadly, the men of Darién realized
that disaster had overtaken the good man and that
another mission must start for Hispaniola and
Spain. Balboa begged to go as their envoy. He
wanted to announce the existence of the unknown
sea and to recruit a thousand men who would fight
their way to it through the kingdom of Tubanamá.
But the colonists would not hear of it: to them he
was indispensable. As envoys they named Colmenares and an older man, Juan de Quecido, the only
settler whose wife had accompanied him. Of both

they demanded guarantees that they would return. Colmenares, who had large plantations, pledged his properties; Quecido left his wife in Darién.

They had a brutal voyage to Hispaniola. A voyage that with a favoring wind took a mere eight days was unmercifully prolonged by late autumn gales and adverse currents. It was a hundred days before they could kneel in a church in Santo Domingo and give thanks for their safe arrival. They lost no time in reporting to Don Diego: They pleaded for recruits and supplies and answered his many questions, speaking fully and freely. From Santo Domingo they took passage on a merchant ship for Spain, arriving there in May, having been seven months on the way. No one in Spain could have thought this unusual or unduly hard. But an eyewitness remarked that Colmenares and Quecido looked "as yellow and puffy as though they suffered from liver complaint." He thought their sickly appearance was not due to the hardships they had suffered but was proof of Darién's unhealthy climate. Whether it was the voyage, ill health, or age, Quecido soon died, leaving Colmenares alone at court to represent Darién—and Balboa.

Colmenares was not a villain; he was honest and

trustworthy. First Nicuesa had relied on him to carry out his orders carefully, and after Nicuesa, Balboa. He was a man who somehow managed to play on the winning team. He had arrived in the New World in the service of Nicuesa. Then he had served under Balboa and again served well. He in particular had been close to Balboa, had been admitted to his secret plans and purposes. More than anyone else, Colmenares appreciated the stature of Balboa, the devotion he had inspired, his concern for the colony's well-being, and, above all, what he had accomplished.

Yet Colmenares never spoke of these matters in Spain. Perhaps he thought it would be useless or dangerous to disagree with Bishop Fonseca, the all-powerful head of the agency set up by the Crown to handle Spanish policy and administration in the New World. By nature Fonseca was a schemer, a very capable man, but a schemer who felt at ease with other schemers; a courtier who led one court faction and distrusted all outside that charmed circle. Dreamers, like Columbus, and doers, like Balboa, are of a different breed—they are the noble solitary stags who are killed by packs of scheming wolves. Fonseca and Enciso had much in common.

What had happened earlier when Enciso and Zamudio first arrived in Spain? They had immediately reported the state of affairs in Darién to Fonseca. Enciso, at home in legal courts and easy of speech, had used pure venom to paint Balboa, calling him a murderer and usurper. Zamudio had plainly called Enciso a liar, charging that he had no valid claim to be mayor of Darién. Enciso, he shouted, held his authority from Ojeda, whereas Darién was located on Nicuesa's grant. His brash manners and defense of Balboa irritated Fonseca, and to save himself from the bishop's hostility, Zamudio had to hide with friends. He was still in hiding when Colmenares arrived with his electrifying news of an unknown sea.

In those days when men were becoming accustomed to the announcement of new lands—each returning ship had discoveries to boast of—it was novel and exciting to be told of the Indians' reports of a new sea. And momentous. Spain had but to take possession of it—formal possession—to have the right to claim sovereignty over all the lands surrounding its waters. Darién—gateway to the unknown sea—would be the choicest prize. He whom the king appointed to rule that province

would enjoy boundless wealth, power, and opportunity. Fonseca did not intend that anything as
important as Darién should go to either Enciso or
Balboa: Darién was a plum he would feed to one of
his favorites.

To Colmenares, Fonseca declared that he had
made up his mind about Balboa. He referred to him
as the stowaway, the usurper, the dangerous adventurer, the lawless bandit. Confronted by this attitude the new envoy knew better than to suggest
that, in the two years since Enciso had left Darién,
Balboa had been none of these things. He knew
Zamudio had gained nothing by blurting out that
it was Balboa who had saved the remnants of the
Ojeda and Nicuesa expeditions and saved Darién.
Colmenares thought it best not to say that Balboa
was asking for men only in order to secure a fabulous treasure for Spain.

With Colmenares silent, Fonesca, whose power
in the New World was second only to King Ferdinand's, continued to describe Balboa in Enciso's
words. To achieve his own end Fonseca would use
Enciso's false claims, not in Enciso's behalf, but as
a weapon against Balboa.

VIII
1513: Balboa's Year

The new year came. Darién celebrated it with the arrival of three ships loaded and dispatched by Don Diego. They were substantial proof of the energetic response the governor of Hispaniola had given to the glorious news of a new sea brought by Colmenares and Quecido. It was natural that Columbus's son should be pleased with a Darién governed by Balboa: unlike Ojeda and Nicuesa, the newcomer would not try to by-pass him. A grateful Balboa might be the means whereby Don Diego could reinstate his father's rights to the lands of the New World. And so as soon as the envoys had embarked for Spain, the governor started collecting whatever Hispaniola could spare. For the colonists' immediate use he sent wine and cheeses, biscuit and bacon; for future needs he sent chickens and pigs, seeds, plants and cuttings. To build up the colony's fighting strength he sent a good assortment of weapons and fighters to handle them—150 spirited volunteers.

The captain of the small fleet handed Balboa two letters. One, which he knelt to receive, bore the royal seal. Signed by Ferdinand himself, it appointed Vasco Nuñez de Balboa temporary governor and acting captain general of the Province of Darién. (Was it Fonseca who had reinforced the king's caution by suggesting that Balboa's authority be provisional?) At last Balboa had received royal recognition. And he was filled with such joy and pride that the sound of his rapidly beating heart had the urgency of church bells announcing a holy day. Then he opened the other letter.

This letter had been smuggled out of Spain and was dated after that from the king. It was from Zamudio. Though he was practically banished from the court and in hiding, Zamudio had been able to keep in touch with what was happening in the highest circles. There, where the source of power lay, the intrigues were most concentrated, alive, and polite. There murder was a matter of a word, a glance, a sad shaking of the head; and the victim, near or far away, was as dead as if he had a dagger in his chest. Or, chained and left to rot in some foul dungeon, the prisoner might long for the swift dispatch of a dagger. Zamudio's was a warning letter.

He described how willingly court officials had listened to Enciso's false account of Balboa's role in the founding of Darién. To different officials he had made different insinuations, cleverly matching his lies to suit their prejudices. Some officials were given to understand that Balboa, a fugitive from the law, had thrown Ojeda and Nicuesa out of Darién in order to seize power. To others Enciso suggested that Balboa was a dangerous rebel who used the safety of an ocean between him and his king to defy the royal wish as it had been stated in the royal grants. Still others considered Balboa a tyrant who forcibly banished anyone who challenged his rule. All, Zamudio warned, agreed with Fonseca who urged that a successor must be appointed, a well-known man who would land with troops and restore law and order. Even now Fonseca was

persuading the king to terminate Balboa's temporary appointment and select a proper governor who
would overthrow that arch rebel, that usurper,
Balboa. Once in their power, they would have Balboa sent back to Spain, stripped of everything, a
powerless prisoner to stand trial for high treason.
They would make certain that another, not Balboa,
would discover the sea and gather the golden
treasure.

Balboa read and reread Zamudio's words and,
knowing Enciso, he believed they rang true. He
was thankful to Zamudio for having given him the
only weapon with which to defend himself: time.
As long as his temporary appointment was effective,
he had time—how long a space of time he did not
know—before a successor appeared. He had time to
cross the mountains; time to be the man to secure
for Spain and his king the new ocean. Let Balboa
but present the South Sea to the king and a gift of
such royal magnitude would silence his enemies and
prove his loyalty—or so he thought, and thinking
so, he knew that he could not afford to wait until he
had the thousand men he had asked for. He would
do great deeds with the slim forces he had. Leading

as large a party as he could muster, he would start his march to the South Sea.

But first he would write his king. He wanted to put into words as well as into actions the reasons and justifications for what he had done in Darién. Everything, he explained, he had done to carry out the king's wishes. Were the king's deepest concerns for the well-being of his people? Did the king desire treasure? These two considerations had guided Balboa's efforts. Addressing the king about the business of exploration, Balboa mentioned how he constantly sought to find gold, silver, pearls—whatever the country produced. He described his vigilance in protecting the king's interests. He itemized the amounts of gold he had already forwarded to the royal treasurer by different messengers at various times. Considerable as these amounts were, they would be counted as paltry when compared with the immense treasure he was about to seek. As every man hungered for gold, so the hunger of the king would be of royal size. Even so huge an appetite would be satisfied by the gold Balboa would find plentifully, easily, by the South Sea.

"The method of collecting gold is without any

labor," he wrote the king, passing on the information he had learned. "One way is to wait for the streams to rise in the ravines, and when the floods pass, the gold remains exposed, washed down from the mountains in very large grains. The Indians indicate they are the size of oranges and like the fist. The other method is to wait until the vegetation on the mountains becomes dry. Then it is set on fire, and after it is burnt, the gold is collected in great quantity and in very beautiful grains."

Without pointing directly at Enciso, he recommended that no lawyers be permitted in the province, entreating the king to keep them out. "No lawyer comes here," he wrote (surely thinking of Enciso and Corral), "who is not a very devil, and they lead the life of devils, and not only are they bad, but they even contrive to bring about a thousand lawsuits and villainies."

Then Balboa wrote that he knew—as every Spaniard knew—of the king's concern for every part of his realm and for the welfare of every one of his subjects. As the man representing the royal authority, he had struggled constantly to see that the colony flourished and that its people were safe and healthy. His words rang with pride in his accomplishments but they also told of his obedience and loyalty. He signed himself "The creature and creation of Your Highness, who kisses your hands and feet."

So he wrote, unaware that Enciso was just a tool being used against him. Control of Darién with its immense promise was now the subject of Court intrigue.

Having written and sealed his letter, Balboa gave his attention to the great adventure ahead.

IX

The March to the South Sea

Balboa carefully looked over the men of Darién. He could not risk using the newcomers Don Diego had sent. They still could not stand up to hardships. Their stomachs, accustomed to better food, were made sick by the native bread, by vegetables cooked without salt, and by river water that was often unwholesome. The men of Darién were veterans hardened to the foods, the hunger and thirst, the clouds of insects, the rain, the oppressive heat, and the Indian way of fighting. From among them he chose the men to accompany him and armed them with all the swords, crossbows, and arquebuses his arsenal could provide. The 190 men he had selected were a closely united, tough, experienced group, ready for any Indian trickery and resourceful when the going was hard. They were fighters whom he knew and had led; they were loyal to him and had learned to trust in his leadership.

"I have chosen you," Balboa said to the assembled men, "to see if one hundred and ninety Spaniards can do what Comogre's son, Carlos, estimated it would take a thousand to accomplish. I can promise you now that we will meet tribes whose warriors are famous for their fierce fighting. We shall be outnumbered many times. But I have thought that if each man fights with the fury of five and we have God's help, we shall be like an army of a thousand. I tell you we shall march either to a dreadful death or to undying glory and untold riches."

He regretted that when they faced the armies of Quarequá and Tubanamá they would not have the help of their horses. The mere sight of men on horseback would have thrown those thousands of painted, shouting warriors into a terrible panic, but hoisting the animals up the steep cliffs would slow them down too much. Balboa preferred the advantage of speed and surprise. They did take their fighting dogs—huge animals like Balboa's own Leoncico—trained to attack Indians as other hunting dogs were trained to jump at the throat of a charging boar or to hamstring a fleeing deer.

They waited for the rainy season to end. The daily downpour turned little streams into raging floods and multiplied the hardships and toil of travel. When the torrential rains were tapering off into occasional showers, Balboa and his men left Darién. It was the first day of September, 1513. They made a brave appearance aboard a brigantine and ten large canoes as they sailed to their starting place, the village of Balboa's friend and father-in-law, Careta. For two pleasant days he consulted with Careta, storing up more valuable information, collecting additional supplies, gaining Indian allies, and making a final choice of the overland party. He selected about one hundred to accompany him and left the rest to protect Careta's village and the Spaniards' own fleet. Then, at the head of his small force and with a guide leading the way, Balboa started the overland march to the South Sea.

Let us stop for a moment and consider this party as it leaves the shore, crosses the steaming, swampy lowlands, and disappears into the forest gloom, determined to explore the interior. Until then no European had deliberately attempted such a step.

In the twenty busy years after Columbus many men had sailed thousands of miles tracing New World coastlines, sifting out the islands from the mainland, seeking a passage to the Orient through the unbroken continental wall. But nowhere had explorers ventured into the interior. It is true that some explorers had steered their fleets into deep bays or a considerable way up rivers, but none had left their ships to do more than land to fill their water barrels. To all these bold explorers and navigators, carried far by winds and currents, their ships were their home away from home. Each ship was a European ark afloat in a strange world.

It is with Balboa that the penetration and exploration of the New World land mass begins. He set up the targets—Mexico and Peru—which Cortés and Pizarro would strike, and he worked out the methods by which they would be conquered. Because Balboa broke a trail through to the Pacific, Spain would later scoop up the treasures of two continents. By following in Balboa's footsteps, Cortés and Pizarro found the empires of the Aztecs and the Incas. As Columbus had opened the gates of the Atlantic, so Balboa was the pioneer who, venturing deep into the unknown land, opened the gates for the explorers who actually burned their ships behind them so that there would be no retreat from the march into the interior.

Balboa's greatest single asset, which he had won by his deep humanity, was his success in dealing with the Indians. Balboa's Indians were not slaves but allies who respected his qualities and responded to his desires, allies who made the march into the interior possible. Indians carried the Spaniards' baggage; used their knowledge of trees and vines to build shelters, rafts, and bridges as they were needed; cooked the food; and fashioned large canoes out of mighty tree trunks. Most important of all, Indian guides led Balboa's men along the jungle trails that brought them through that unknown land. From Balboa's time on, whether it was Spanish, English, French, or American explorers who advanced into the interior, they relied on Indian knowledge and Indian help. The method had not changed three hundred years later when Lewis and Clark crossed the wide heartland of North America to the Pacific.

And so Balboa's party left the steaming, swampy
lowlands and headed for the mountains. Immediately the jungle swallowed them. They could not
see ahead to judge how distant were the mountains
which they would have to climb and, looking back,
they could not see where they had entered and how
far they had come.

For two days they advanced over jagged, hilly
country until they came to a clearing where Ponca,
the chief who had fled from them before, had established his village and fields. Again Ponca fled, but
this time Balboa was not playing the chief's game
of hide-and-seek: he could not leave an enemy between himself and his base on the coast. Balboa sent
messengers inviting Ponca to return to his own
village and be the friend and ally of the Spaniards.
The Indian, who had seen how honorably Balboa
treated his friends and had tasted the punishment
he inflicted on an enemy, welcomed the chance
offered him. He returned to his village where he
treated Balboa as his guest and friend. Both leaders
were delighted with their new alliance. Ponca
sealed his friendship with a large gift of gold. He
wished that he had more to give, but most of his
gold, he said, the Spaniards had taken when they

last visited his village. Balboa matched Ponca's present with the European goods that the Indians fancied—necklaces of glass beads, mirrors, copper bells, and steel needles—and won Ponca's gratitude when he added some iron hatchets, the article most valued and desired. So princely a gift won Balboa Ponca's offer to furnish him with guides and bearers. The men Careta had sent to serve in these capacities were dismissed with generous presents. Balboa felt so certain of Ponca's good will that he left a dozen Spaniards who, too ill to continue, were to remain there to be cared for and, when they had recovered, were to be guided back to Careta's village.

Having thus secured his line of retreat and freed the party from the burden of men too sick to keep up the fast pace, Balboa left Ponca on September 20. He pushed resolutely toward the unknown. Almost immediately the mountains tested the Spaniards' will to conquer. They reared up, a succession of sharp, steep, jagged cliffs. For four days each step was a challenge to stout hearts and sure feet. They lifted themselves up slippery precipices, cut a path through tree-tangled slopes. Up and up they scrambled in the darkness of the forest floor.

Thundering cascades forced long detours. Foaming mountain streams were crossed on swaying bridges of twisted vines. For four days they sweated and puffed, slipping, sliding, but always climbing until they reached the mountain kingdom of the invincible Chief Quarequá.

So secure was Quarequá in his high mountain kingdom that no sentries had been posted to warn him of the coming of the powerful white chief of Darién. Balboa had been told that Quarequá's power lay in his strategic location—he held the key to transit across the Isthmus—and that before the Spaniard could claim the South Sea he would have to conquer Quarequá.

And so they met and took stock of each other. To Quarequá, the undisputed master of that region, the Spaniards were intruders who would feel his might. To Balboa this Indian chief was the main obstacle to the goal he sought. And as he looked at the chief surrounded by his war leaders and backed by a thousand warriors, Quarequá spoke. "Retrace your steps if you do not wish to be killed to the last man!"

While the sound of his words still filled the silence between them the two groups faced one another. The Spaniards, now less than seventy, had put on their metal helmets and corselets; they stood, their swords drawn, the crossbows fixed, the arquebuses primed. At their feet lay their dogs, trained to war, waiting the signal to jump at the throats of the Indians. Behind them Ponca's men, the guides and bearers, watched to see if their new friends could shatter the power of Quarequá, whose name spelled terror and whose warriors had never known defeat.

The Spaniards looked on the large force blocking their path and marveled. Quarequá and his nobles, in the insignia of their high rank, seemed to be sheathed in skins of gold that glittered under the sunlight. Large pieces of gold plate, beautifully worked and fitted, covered their arms and chests. The rest of their naked bodies was protected by wooden shields covered with animal skins. Their weapons were huge two-handed wooden swords, bows and arrows, and fire-hardened, sharp-pointed wooden lances. Hurled with power and deadly aim from a throwing stick, they could pass these lances clean through the bodies of their enemies. The Indians stood confident of their vast superiority of numbers, of their death-dealing javelins, of the power of their priests who called the gods to fight by beating drums and blowing conch shells. They knew nothing of the Spaniards' lethal gunpowder, nor their steel that could sever bone.

Led by Quarequá, the great body of Indians, whooping and shrilling their battle cries, ran toward the intruders as though to drown them under waves of warriors. The Spaniards steadied and then fired point-blank. Stunned by the lightning and thunder that killed and wounded men at a distance, the Indians stopped, and standing thus were drenched by the shower of the crossbowmen's arrows. More fell dead or wounded. Then the slaughter began. The terrified Indians did not know which way to run to escape. Those who ran backward were brought down by the bloodhounds that leaped for their throats; those who advanced were cut to ribbons by the Spaniards. Possessed by the fury of battle, the Spaniards swung their sharp steel swords like cleavers, hacking off arms and legs, severing heads. Slashing, hacking, cutting, they covered the ground with the dead. It was butchery, not a battle. Quarequá, all his nobles, and most of his warriors were slain.

It was soon over. The terrible slaughter marked

the triumph of gunpowder and steel; not a Spaniard was killed and only a few had suffered slight
wounds. The natives who survived could not understand how their world, so safe, so powerful, so
rich, had perished in one morning. They watched the
Spaniards enter their village and systematically
search every house for gold. What they found was
added to the great pile of golden breastplates and
arm bands, heavy polished ear plugs, and delicately
cast nose plugs that Balboa's men had already
stripped from the dead.

Balboa knew that their victory had been so
complete that it would be quite safe to leave the
sick and wounded in that mountain village where
they could recuperate. He also knew that he could
command the allegiance of these newly made captives to serve faithfully as guides and bearers. Dis-
missing Ponca's men, he sent them back with
presents; they could hardly wait to rush down the
mountain to announce Balboa's overwhelming
victory.

At last the Spaniards could put down their arms
and eat and rest in Quarequá's village. The tropic
night came suddenly and it was very cold.

X

The South Sea

The next morning, only waiting for the dawn to light their way, Balboa's party took the trail. He wanted to see if Comogre's son had spoken truly, if indeed from the peak of a nearby mountain the South Sea was visible. Soon the guide pointed to a bare, rocky summit—the Sierra of Quarequá, as it was called. Balboa bade his men wait while alone, with only his dog as company, he climbed. A few more steps and the doubt that had haunted him would be forever quieted. He would know if he had spent his men, his time, and his strength on legends and lies. A moment more, a few steps more, and he was at the last rise. Now his eyes would know whether the venture was to be crowned with success. He reached the summit and looked. There was the sea!

The sight he saw brought him to his knees—a heavenly blue shimmering with the gold and silver of the midmorning sun. He was gazing on an arm of the sea, the mighty sea, reaching deep into the forested land. He saluted the South Sea, the promised sea, whose existence proclaimed his success, his fame, his fortune. He saluted this sea unknown to Europe and now known to the eyes of one European, Balboa. His heart beat wildly as he poured out his boundless gratitude to God that He had reserved this glory for him. Then he beckoned to his men so that he might show them a sea heretofore unknown to the inhabitants of the kingdoms of Europe.

"Behold the much desired ocean. Behold! All you men who have shared such efforts, behold the country of which the son of Comogre and all the others told us such wonders! And as they spoke truly of this, so they spoke truly of the great riches we shall find." And the Spaniards knelt and sang a hymn of praise and thankfulness. To mark the spot they heaped up stones into an altar and planted on it a

cross into which the letters F and J were carved. "In the name of Castile and Aragon"—to Ferdinand the Regent, and his daughter, Queen Juana, they dedicated this peak which gave Europeans their first glimpse of the South Sea. The gift Balboa would give his king-to-be, Charles V, the son of the mad Juana, was possession of the vast Pacific with dominion over all its lands and seas "as long as the world endures, and unto the final day of judgment of all mankind."

This ceremony enacted four hundred and fifty years ago, the morning of September 25, 1513, on a peak in the province of Darién, was written down as it happened; and the notary, who certified to the discovery of the South Sea, listed the sixty-seven men who stood beside the altar.

There was nothing unusual in such a procedure. From the time Queen Isabella helped finance Christopher Columbus's first voyage, the Spanish Crown guarded their stake in the many expeditions that set out to explore the New World. Businesslike, they maintained business methods.

Records were kept of items supplied: weapons, foodstuffs, horses, plants—everything and anything furnished to the expeditions was carefully entered. Persons taking part in the great adventures were listed. Copies of letters sent out and the letters received were filed. Every item, every event—the number of cheeses sent to Darién or the discovery of the South Sea—was certified by a notary. In the picture of the Spanish conquistador which history shows us there is always a friar close by, for the Cross and the Crown advanced together. But outside the picture, though perhaps just as close, walked the notary, the agent of the king, with his ledgers and records.

It was midday, so the notary wrote, when Balboa took his last look at the sea and started down the trail that would lead out of the mountains, through the forest, to the shore of the South Sea.

Almost immediately his advance was challenged by Chiapes, a warlike chief, through whose territory the Spaniards had to pass. Like Quarequá, on the other side of the divide, Chiapes, with his proud warriors behind him, thought to stop this small band of men who seemed so weak and tired. Again the arquebuses blazed with fire and noise, again the dogs were unleashed to leap and tear, again the chief and his nobles fled while the people fell to the ground too terrified to stand before such supernatural displays. In a few minutes the Spanish were masters and Balboa ordered his men to stop. He did not want dead Indians; he wanted friends. He needed allies. As he had offered friendship to Ponca, so now he sent messengers to Chiapes to induce the frightened chief to return. Presents were exchanged —this time the Spaniards received pearls—and by this alliance Balboa extended his chain of friends to the western side of the mountains. He decided to rest for a few days where it was so pleasant and cool and to wait for the sick and wounded he had left behind to rejoin the main party. He paid off the guides and sent them back with messages for the Spaniards.

While waiting he sent out patrols to find the nearest way to the sea. One of the groups suddenly came upon two canoes. The men stood there, wondering, discussing the meaning of two canoes on dry land, when their sharp ears heard a sound. Was it the leaves rustling? A far-off whisper? An ambush? Ready for any action, they were not prepared for what they saw: the powerful Pacific tide, many times higher and stronger than the tides they had at Darién. It seemed to gobble up the dry field and soon the canoes were afloat.

At this news Balboa took twenty-six men who had regained their strength and followed the trail to the sea. The forest ended sharply. One step separated the deep shade from the hot sun and he saw a wide-open space, the same tree-ringed bay empty of water. He went no farther but stepped back into the cool forest: He had but to wait for the tide to bring the sea to his feet. It came, a ripple of water pushed toward the forest and, behind it, the sea returning to its bay. Balboa was ready with ceremony and word to claim the mighty ocean for the Spanish Crown.

Holding a precious banner brought especially for this solemn act—the Virgin and Child smiling above the arms of Castile and Aragon—Balboa, with buckler fastened and sword drawn, waded into the bay until the water covered his knees. He pronounced the resounding phrases of the formula used in taking possession. And as he spoke, so the notary wrote the claim; and to the document the men signed their names as witnesses. They too had waded into the bay, tasted the water, and found in its salty taste the proof that it was an ocean they had discovered. Into the trunks of trees whose roots ran far out into the water they carved three great crosses—one for the Father, one for the Son, and one for the Holy Ghost. Thus they included land and water in their sacred ceremony. It was September 29, 1513, and in honor of the saint's feast day Balboa named the bay after San Miguel.

A month had passed since Balboa had led his party out of Darién, a month of hardship, misery, and stunning successes. The Spaniards had crossed the Isthmus. They had spent eighteen days on a trail each foot of which had been hacked out of a tangled mass of suffocating vegetation. They had slipped and slithered in the churned-up black mud or pasted themselves against water-smooth cliffs and painfully inched their way up: eighteen days of exhausting work, eighteen nights passed in a cramped numbness. Crossing the jagged cordillera —as the Spaniards called parallel chains of mountains—had left them aching with a fatigue that was forgotten in the exciting view of the new sea and the taste of its saltiness. Now with a sense of great accomplishment, in the quiet and ease and security of the village of his new friend, Chiapes, Balboa and his men relaxed and rested.

They had collected much gold. So much gold that its weight was becoming a burden, and they smiled when they grumbled at having to carry it. Now they were excited by the pearls Chiapes had offered them—ah! so many and most marvelous, as light as bubbles and as precious as gold. Chiapes told Balboa that his pearls had come from the land of a nearby chief.

The search for pearls soon brought the Spaniards to the coastal territory of another chief named Tumaco, whom Balboa also gained as a friend. When, in the ceremonial exchange of gifts to cement friendship, Tumaco saw the joy and amazement that the sight of the pearls produced, he sent his men out to dive for more and to his first generous gift he added more baskets heaped with pearls of all shapes and sizes and of great beauty and value. When Balboa saw Tumaco's state canoe with its paddle handles studded royally with pearls, he ordered the notary to record the fact and certify to its truth.

From amiable talks with Chiapes and Tumaco, Balboa learned what he could of the lands around the South Sea. The finest pearls came from islands a day's hard paddle to the west. Dites, chief of those islands, controlled the coastal waters and, when the sea was calm, he sent his navy of canoes

to raid their mainland villages. They also confirmed
what Comogre's son had said about a mighty nation
to the south. They spoke with awe of its great
wealth and greater might, of its ocean-going canoes
equipped with sails, and of a strange pack animal
that refused to carry riders. To show what this
unique beast was like, Tumaco made a clay figure:
the body of a sheep, four legs, and a foolishly long
neck. So Spaniards first heard of the llama of Peru.
Cousin to the camel, they thought it was a camel,
and took its existence to be an indication that Asia
was near. Two of the men who thus heard of the
wealth and might of Peru lived to find their way to
that Andean kingdom ruled by the Incas: One of
them, standing beside Balboa, was Pizarro.

In quiet days and stirring talk another month
passed. The party had amassed pounds of gold and
bushels of pearls. They had made firm friends and
learned from them of other chiefs and other kingdoms.

It was time, Balboa knew, to recross the mountains and from Darién announce his discoveries to
the world.

XI
The Long Road Back to Darién

By destroying Quarequá, by making alliances
with Chiapes and Ponca, Balboa had kept the road
back to Darién open and safe. He could have made
a quick return by retracing the outward path. But
he wanted to explore more of this unknown land,
take new trails, meet new tribes in fight or friendship, and locate new treasures. Chiapes and Tumaco
provided him with provisions. They gave him
canoes and paddlers to take the party up the river
that knifed through the great forest to the territory of an inland chief, Teoca. Only the healthy
and strong accompanied Balboa. The others re-

mained in Chiapes' village to be cared for until they could rejoin the main party. Chiapes himself and Tumaco's son went as guides and envoys. Thus Teoca was advised of the gifts of gold which would make his friendship acceptable to this invincible white chief.

At Teoca's village Balboa said farewell to Chiapes and to Tumaco's son. They wept unashamedly as they took their leave and started for home. And those tears, genuine tears, were a tribute to a man who could win the trust and loyalty of those he conquered. And so for a month, watched over and provided for by Indian friends, Balboa's party wandered through the high mountain country. At the Indians' insistence he destroyed a chief whom they abominated and made far-reaching alliances that tied Teoca's lands to him and his rule. On December 1, Balboa's whole group was reunited and they started the long journey back.

Before them was a wide region, empty and without water. The dry season had caused the rivers to disappear. The stream they followed ended as a dry gash in the cliff, leaving a harsh canyon out of which they had to pull themselves. For four days they marched and then came to a forest where they would have perished of thirst had not the Indians found little springs hidden under some trees. Even the forest floor was caked and dry. It was a nightmare country, where dusty channels reminded them of flowing water, where gloomy valleys held treacherous quicksand marshes. Across it, slowly, wearily, they toiled: always thirsty, often hungry, and carrying more treasure than Europe had ever seen collected by one man.

And so, struggling and straggling along the trail, they came to the village of Chief Pocorosa. It was empty of people but stocked with food and blessed with water. Again Balboa sent messengers to find the chief, and when he and his people had returned, the ceremony of alliance took place. It was from him that the Spaniards learned that but two days' journey away was the village of Tubanamá. Here at last was the king known to Comogre's son, Carlos, known far and wide for his evil ways and great wealth, the lord of the mountain country whose armies even a thousand soldiers could not conquer. Pocorosa added that he was cruel and feared and allowed no one to enter his territory and live. Here was a challenge Balboa could not afford to disregard. While pacifying and conciliating the native tribes, he had learned that often the enemy of his newest ally must be dealt with. Yet his men were thin from hunger and pale with exhaustion. How was the crucial test to be met?

Weeding out the weakest, Balboa was left with a force of seventy—not a thousand, but seventy! He wondered if his Spaniards, with their disciplined training, their superior weapons, and their careful schooling in conquest, could force Tubanamá to meet them on their own terms. Briefly he explained the situation and his plan.

"The chief Tubanamá has been boasting widely that he is our implacable enemy and will not let us through his territory alive. He knows, as we know, that our way home lies across his country. It is my opinion that if we surprise him before he can collect his warriors, we can subdue him. This means that we shall have to cover the two-day march in one." This they did.

Just after night had fallen, when Tubanamá's subjects and allies had scattered to their settlements, the Spaniards, assisted by Pocorosa's warriors, fell on Tubanamá's own village. It contained only two long, grass-roofed houses. In one, Tubanamá and his eighty wives lived; the other, now empty, housed his warriors only when they were gathered to make war. Thus, without a fight, the dread tiger of the mountains and his wives were captured.

Again Balboa showed his genius for dealing with Indians: He suited his action to the man. He did not kill Tubanamá as he had Quarequá. Neither did he permit so important a chief to slip into a friendly alliance by the customary exchange of gifts. First he humiliated him. Tubanamá, fearing he was to be killed, threw himself at Balboa's feet and begged for mercy. Then Balboa stripped him of his store of gold by levying a fine as the price of his life. Finally, when he was humbled and penitent, Tubanamá was admitted to Balboa's friendship. That it was friendship Balboa eventually inspired can be seen in Tubanamá's giving one of his sons to his captor for him to rear as a Christian.

One of Balboa's companions watched this new procedure. He saw how Tubanamá's subjects brought in all their gold when they thought their chief's life depended on the amount of the offering. Pocorosa's men had told them that the Spaniards' good will fed on this yellow metal. Pizarro watched the glittering pile grow as thousands of golden necklaces, arm bands, bracelets, and nose plugs were collected from all the villages and brought to the waiting Spaniards. Later, in Peru, Pizarro would use this method to secure the fabulous wealth of the Incas.

December: the year was ending. Balboa and his men returned to Pocorosa's village to get everything in order. Reunited for the return trip, the men thought longingly of Darién where, after so great and continuous an effort, they could rest. And then, when the peril and risks and forced exertions were almost over, Balboa fell ill. Along with the others who were too weak to walk he was carried by Indians in a hammock suspended from a pole. By slow, easy stages the party followed the downward trail to Comogre's village. Comogre had died and Carlos, who had spurred them on to their discoveries and adventures, was now chief. He went out to meet his noble friend. When he found Balboa too spent to walk, and he saw how thin and wan the others were, his hospitality grew greater, his friendship more attentive. For four days he nursed them, giving them the best food his gardens offered, the most nourishing drinks he could brew. He provided them with rest and quiet so that undisturbed they could sleep out their weariness.

Balboa had a deep affection for this Indian youth because of the bright courage he had shown when they first met. Now he loved him for the solicitude with which he tended the many sick and helpless Spaniards who crowded him out of his village and ate up his stores of fresh food. Balboa gave him gifts he knew Carlos would value—hatchets and a complete set of carpenters' tools. He also gave him personal presents—his soldier's cloak and one of his shirts—which the Indian would proudly treasure.

On January 17, 1514, Balboa was welcomed by the village of his father-in-law, Careta, four and a half months after he had started out on an overland journey into the unknown. Not a single man had been lost. Balboa knew the magnitude of his accomplishment: He had left the coast, bent on a desperate venture; he returned, having led an immortal enterprise. With pride, with truth, with unexpected humor, he could tell Careta, "We have more gold than health."

XII

The Secret Mission
of Pedro de Arbolancha

Good luck attended Balboa's homecoming. The brigantine he had left at Careta's village carried him swiftly to Darién, where he was gladdened to see four ships, well-laden, newly arrived from Hispaniola. A few days later, when the rest of the expedition had arrived and the settlers were reunited, the entire population celebrated a solemn high mass. One and all, they thanked God for the explorers' safe return and the magnitude of their success.

Then they turned to the serious business of di-

viding the booty. Everything was displayed for all
to see, to count, to examine, to admire: gold and
pearls; an assortment of useful articles made out of
cotton—hammocks, robes, bags and lengths of
woven goods; and a large number of captives, both
men and women. While everyone watched and the
notary stood by with his lists that recorded each
man's rank and service, the delicate task of appor-
tioning began. First Balboa set aside the royal fifth,
adding as a gift to the king two hundred of the
largest and finest pearls. Then each member of the
expedition received his share; and since even the
dogs had contributed to their victories, the dogs
would be rewarded. Finally the men of Darién and
those who had remained at Careta's village were
each presented with cotton goods or captives.

So fair, so open, so reasonable, was Balboa's
method and division that everyone felt satisfied.
There was no disgruntled whispering, no secret
enviousness. Now they could look forward to new
and equally great conquests. Even Corral and Rua
and their turncoat followers, who had plotted
against Balboa, shared in the fruits of the enterprise; they were grateful that Balboa had not har-

bored ill will toward them. The men of Darién congratulated themselves that they had a leader as able and energetic and just as Balboa.

One man watched these events with special interest: Pedro de Arbolancha. The people of Darién knew him as the agent in charge of the shiploads of food and supplies brought from Hispaniola. He had assumed that position to cover up his real role. Secretly, without even Fonseca's knowledge, the king had dispatched Arbolancha to his farthest outpost to investigate the state of affairs there. His orders were to observe Balboa closely, to ascertain whether he was a usurper who would try to prevent the landing of the new governor sent out to replace him. Had Balboa seized power? Was he a tyrant whom the colonists feared? Was he promoting his own ambition or the welfare of the colony? The questions to which the king wanted answers voiced the doubts and fears about Balboa's conduct that had been set in motion by Enciso's accusations.

The aged Ferdinand of Spain was too experienced in ruling and too suspicious of intrigues not to know how personal envy and enmity could distort facts. He did not want to have to look at Darién and Balboa only through Enciso's eyes; he wanted another opinion before deciding what manner of man the colonists had chosen as leader. The king knew Arbolancha—on previous missions he had found him honest, intelligent, and discreet— and valued his judgment.

Arriving at Darién shortly before Balboa's triumphant return, Arbolancha had the perfect opportunity to question the settlers about many matters that directly and indirectly brought them to talk about their absent leader. If he congratulated them on their well-tended gardens, they would tell him how Balboa had set them an example by working in the fields. If he commented on the slaves and women each settler had to keep his house, they would relate how Balboa had distributed captives among all the settlers. He was, they would add, always concerned for their welfare, always fair, never taking advantage of his position for his own gain. What he had he had won by his enterprise and courage.

Arbolancha was on hand to witness Balboa's arrival. He saw the welcome, a genuine, warm outpouring of affection for a returned hero. He was pleased at the way the booty was divided—in other, less capable hands, greed and distrust would have set every man against his neighbor and started fights. Most of all he marveled that Balboa had extended the peace and good will within the colony to the Indians, making allies of neighboring chiefs. He met Tubanamá's son who was already speaking Spanish and had been baptized a Christian; yet the colonists had said that it was but six months ago that his father had boasted of his hatred of the Spaniards. Convinced by all he had seen and heard, Arbolancha knew that Balboa was indeed a remarkable man worthy of the king's trust and support. He would tell the king faithfully and fully that he admired Balboa and give him solid reasons for his admiration.

At last, after many postponements, Arbolancha was ready to return to Spain. To his safekeeping Balboa entrusted a letter to the king announcing his great discoveries, and for the king's pleasure and as a sample of the wealth of the lands by the South Sea, he filled a golden casket with the choicest huge pearls. So well had the secret purpose of Arbolancha's visit been kept that Balboa had no idea that his letter would be placed directly in the king's own hands.

This letter, Arbolancha's glowing report, and

the store of gold and pearls dispatched to the king changed the attitude of the Spanish Crown toward Balboa overnight. This was exactly as Balboa had hoped it would be. His name and his exploits were transmitted not by newspapers but by letters sent to great personages all over Europe. The Pope was informed of the receipt of Balboa's letter "written in military style and informing us that he had crossed the mountain chains dividing our ocean from the hitherto unknown South Sea. No letter," the writer went on to say, "was ever written in prouder language. Not only is Vasco Nuñez reconciled to the Catholic King, who was formerly vexed with him, but he now enjoys the highest favor. For the King has loaded him with privileges and honors and has rewarded his daring exploits."

King Ferdinand immediately named Vasco Nuñez de Balboa *adelantado*, or governor, of the Coast of the South Sea, making legal and official the position Balboa's deeds had won him. The royal decree had a single—but fatal—flaw. Was it at Fonseca's suggestion that the region known as Coast of the South Sea was made part of the Province of Darién, thereby placing Balboa under the jurisdiction of the governor of Darién? For this important post, assigned in the months before Arbolancha's return, while the king was still vexed, had been given to Fonseca's candidate, Pedrarias Dávila.

A slim margin of time mocked Balboa. The old chroniclers recorded that the fleet bearing the newly appointed governor to Darién passed the ship bringing Arbolancha back to Spain. If Arbolancha had arrived in Spain before Pedrarias left, the suspicion, the nagging hostility and ill will, which Enciso had generated and Fonseca had endowed with the terrible power of authority, would not have crossed the Atlantic to hamper Balboa. If—ah! then what a tale of discovery and glory there would have been.

XIII
How Darién Became
Castilla del Oro

A great armada of fifteen ships carried Pedrarias Dávila and his men to their post in the New World. It was the last expedition Ferdinand of Spain sent out and the first organized by the Casa de Contratación, the name of the office created to handle Spain's activities in the New World. When England later planted her American colonies, she too would have similar offices. For behind even the noblest of colonial ventures—whether that of the Pilgrims in Massachusetts or the Quakers in Pennsylvania— were ledgers which itemized the cost of transporting the settlers, of maintaining them until they became self-supporting, and of defending them against Indians incited and armed by European rivals. On the profit side, the Spanish colonies paid their way with shining cargoes of gold and silver and pearls; the English would make theirs pay by means of less glamorous but equally valuable fish and furs.

The king had instructed Fonseca to secure the best people and equipment available. Skilled pilots were attracted by good pay; merchants and traders were given special privileges. Carpenters, blacksmiths, leatherworkers, and tailors, given free passage for their wives and families, were induced to bring their skills to the New World. Spain sent the finest weapons and military supplies as well as great stores of tools and utensils: axes, shovels, chisels, hammers, saws, nails, pots, pans, and roasting spits. She also provided the large expedition with quantities of staple foods: flour and biscuit, dried peas and beans, wine, oil, vinegar, honey, and salt.

Castilla del Oro: Golden Castile. So Darién, despised for its heathen, Indian name, was now christened; it had the sound of a Never-Never Land. And so it was. In Spain men had no ears for grim, sordid experiences but only eyes for the gold and silver loot shipped back from the New World. They easily persuaded themselves that Darién was no name for a city of gold rising above a beach of pearls and they ignored the reality of the poor, needy Indian settlement which the Spaniards had made their base. They forgot that swamps and forests and mountain chains lay between the Spanish base and the places where the treasure had been amassed. The make-believe which colored all their hopes and plans would become a poison in the real Darién. Neither Enciso nor Colmenares, it should be noted, were consulted when Castilla del Oro was named.

Golden Castile was given a government worthy of its name. To assist the new governor, Pedrarias Dávila, other officials with important titles and high salaries were appointed: a treasurer and an auditor to handle financial affairs, a judge and an inspector to enforce the laws, and for the colonists' health a surgeon and a pharmacist. Alongside this civil government there was a religious one, equally impressive, to serve and supervise the community's spiritual needs—a bishop and eight priests. All officials, civil and religious, were to be paid for by Castilla del Oro. At this point their fairy tale was made practical.

Castilla del Oro invited other changes. Because Pedrarias Dávila's wife, Doña Isabel, insisted on going to this post, and because the couple were known for their love of elegant living, the law prohibiting the colonists wearing silks and brocades was lifted. Doña Isabel packed her fine court clothes and her silver plate for dining in state in Golden Castile. The recruits tried to match the opulence of the Dávilas, spending freely to outfit themselves with rich armor and silken finery that they might glitter and gleam as was expected of future citizens of Castilla del Oro.

When Spaniards heard that Comogre's son had suggested that an army of a thousand men should storm Tubanamá's stronghold, applicants for the dazzling opportunity swamped the Casa de Contratación. Ferdinand was forced to raise the number of recruits to two thousand. Among them were several who made their names immortal. Darién was their testing ground and training place; at Darién, it can be said, they went to school to learn from Balboa—the one man who could teach them —the art of advancing into the unknown interior. There De Soto had his first taste of the New World.

Sent afterward with Pizarro to Peru, he made a fortune and was rewarded with the right to rule and exploit Florida, as the entire southeast part of North America was then called. It was as *adelantado* of Florida that he advanced from the Georgia coast to the Mississippi River.

Another was Almagro, who, having participated in the conquest of Peru, went from there overland to conquer Chile. Another was Belalcázar, who looted the gold of Quito and Popayán. Not all were conquistadores. There was Serrano, the chief pilot of the fleet, who later sailed with Magellan and died fighting at his side. And the notary, Oviedo, the official in charge of smelting and marking the gold and branding the slaves, who wrote a monumental work that told of the marvels of the New World— its people, plants, and animals—and how the Spanish conducted themselves. And also—many consider him the greatest chronicler of all—the common soldier Bernal Díaz del Castillo who, born the year of Columbus's first voyage, was to follow Cortés on all his expeditions. When he was eighty-five, Bernal Díaz would tell the amazing story of the conquest of Mexico with candor and genius.

"I have no wealth to leave my sons and descendants," the old man wrote, "but this my truthful and noteworthy narrative."

Pedrarias enjoyed his important role. Head of this most dazzling of expeditions, governor of Castilla del Oro, loyal servant of the king, he promised himself that he would punish the lawless ruffian, Balboa. In July of 1513 he received his commission; in August he appeared before the Royal Council to take the oath of loyalty and obedience; and then for eight months he delayed, though he was scolded by the king for his snail's pace. Month after month enormous amounts of equipment were brought to the docks and loaded on the ships. But Colmenares, who had been called on for advice because he knew the actual conditions in Darién, wanted more supplies. Soberly he warned that so large a number of newcomers would strain the settlement's resources. And as month followed month the recruits waited and, waiting, borrowed against their golden expectations in the New World to pay for food and lodging in Spain.

At last the day of embarkation came. Pedrarias and his officials at the head of a parade—everyone wearing his bravest garments, everyone walking

with light, proud step, and everyone flushed with the excitement of the long-awaited farewell—marched splendidly through the town of Seville, down to the docks. It was April, 1514.

It took the fleet eleven weeks—"sometimes with good weather and other times with bad weather," as Bernal Díaz calmly explains the unusually long crossing—to reach Darién.

On the way they passed the ship bringing Arbolancha to Spain; with him came the magnificent news that Balboa had toppled Tubanamá and discovered the South Sea.

XIV
Pedrarias Dávila

In Spain, Pedrarias's nickname had been "the Gallant." It stuck to him because he was gay and showy in his dress and gay and attentive to the ladies. These were his most noteworthy traits; these and Fonseca's friendship won him the coveted governorship of Castilla del Oro. When his appointment was announced, there had been an outcry: his faults, his foolishness, his deficiencies, made his choice for the position an insult to the cause of Spain. But Fonseca silenced all the complaints. "Pedrarias, O Most Catholic Majesty," he addressed the king, "is a brave man who has often risked his

life for Your Majesty and is well adapted to com-
manding troops. He distinguished himself in the
war against the Moors as a valiant soldier and pru-
dent officer. In my opinion it would be ungracious
to withdraw his appointment in response to the
accusations made against him by envious persons.
Let this good man depart, under the good fortune
of your protection; let this devoted pupil of Your
Majesty, who has lived from infancy in the palace,
depart."

That Fonseca's grand speech won the day for
Pedrarias and silenced his critics showed how little
the Spanish Court had learned from the costly mis-
takes of Ojeda and Nicuesa. The only worthwhile
qualifications were still thought to be those of the
courtier: Family position and vanity still counted
for more than competence and character.

The man who in Spain was scornfully called "the
Gallant" earned another nickname for himself in
the New World: "The Wrath of God." In Spain he
had hidden his stupidity and sour nature under
elegant clothes and an insolent manner; in the New
World his finery looked foolish, and his manner, no
longer the insolence of a private person, became the
arrogance of a disappointed official.

amid the golden riches of Castilla del Oro? Yet
he was, a poorly dressed, quiet, dignified man
nly doing his best to serve them. Was this hut
ounded by a hodgepodge of smaller leaf-
ched huts the fair city of the New World main-
l?

he brave dreams of Castilla del Oro melted
he hot, humid, swampy valley of Darién. The
t few days increased the newcomers' loathing
the place: There was a prevailing smell of putrid
sh gas, and clouds of mosquitoes gave them
peace; filthy water filled whatever well they
; toads were in the very water with which slaves
nkled the dirt floors; lightning licked at men
ping in their beds and bats sucked their blood.
ers were everywhere—in the water they drank,
he air they breathed. Within a month after they
arrived, seven hundred of the eager, exquisitely
ssed recruits were dead. Hundreds more sailed
ck to Hispaniola, since, like Diaz, they felt
here was nothing left to conquer, for Balboa had
nquered it all, and the land is of itself very short."
few had enough to pay their way back to Spain.
ose who had their health had lost their hopes.
The repugnance Pedrarias felt for Darién as it

The sight of Darién was a shock to the man who
had thought of the settlement as Castilla del Oro.
Furthermore Balboa's behavior upset Pedrarias's
plans. For long months before he sailed and for the
eleven weeks of his voyage, the governor had
dreamed of landing by force and overcoming a
surly, dangerous rebel. How could Pedrarias show
off his bravery and fighting skill when there was
nothing to capture and no enemy to fight? For
Balboa with all his council knelt before the new
governor and promised obedience from himself and
the men of Darién, and then to Doña Isabel and
Pedrarias Dávila he graciously offered the use of his
own house. Instead of a victory march, Pedrarias
had to be content with a stately procession. Holding his wife's hand as though for a formal dance,
and with the bishop beside him in his rich robes,
the new governor led his officials and knights, all
fully armed. Behind them walked brown-robed
monks carrying crosses and swinging censers;
bringing up the rear were sailors, skilled workmen,
colonists: the men and women who had filled the
fleet.

The Indians watched this noble promenade with
awe. But the men of Darién—their faces lean from

their poor diet and sallow from fevers, dressed simply and comfortably in cotton shirts and drawers and wearing rope sandals—the men of Darién pitied the newcomers in their silks and brocades, their plumed hats and high leather boots. They knew that many of these people would soon be dead and many more would wish to die.

The dinner Balboa gave to honor his distinguished guests showed most sharply the differences between the men of Darién and the dandies who had sailed for Castilla del Oro. In his house, which had formerly belonged to Cémaco, the chief of the Darién Indians, the two groups sat on the floor with the food heaped up between them: native fruits and roots, cassava bread, maize. To quench their thirst there was river water. For Balboa and his men the quantity of food made this a feast; to the newcomers what was offered either amazed or disgusted them. Many did not even try to taste what had been obtained after hard work and against severe odds. The meal passed in silence. The residents looked at the new officials and felt that the new government would make their hard life harder; the newcomers were stunned by what they saw. Had they not been told that Balboa was a crude upstart who lolled in

was, instead of the imaginary Castilla del Oro of his dreams, settled into a terrible hatred for the man who had robbed him of the glory of planting the flag of Castile on the South Sea. For having deprived him of the fame he yearned for, Pedrarias would make Balboa suffer.

XV
Balboa and Pedrarias

The next two years are but darkly seen. Great events took place on the South Sea. Everyone in Darién knew about them. But Balboa did not live to write their details and meaning to the king. For though the king had officially recognized Balboa's achievements by creating him *adelantado* of the Coast of the South Sea, his post was under the control of Darién's Governor Pedrarias.

As soon as Balboa could leave Darién he started on the task he had planned during the long lazy days spent resting in Chiapes's village. When he had tried to reach the Pearl Islands a gale had forced

his frail canoes back to shore. Now he was determined to build a small but seaworthy ship and sail
out on the South Sea to discover not only the
pearl-rich islands but also the wealthy kingdom his
Indian friends had spoken of with great awe—the
land where the camel-like beast was to be found.

Balboa was the very first to build seagoing ships
in the New World. Because his father-in-law,
Careta, convinced him that certain trees that grew
on his territory were so bitter that even the *broma,*
the sea worm, would not eat them, Balboa decided
to cut his timbers there and transport them across
the mountains to the South Sea. Near Careta's
village he established the Spanish town of Acla
where he felled the trees and cut the heavy timbers
to build four ships. When this was done he and a
few Spaniards supervising hundreds of Indians
transported all the heavy, clumsy equipment—
anchors, rigging, pitch, and tackle—through the
jungle, across waterfalls and rushing mountain
streams, up the steep cliffs, up, up, up over the
mountains. Many Indians wore themselves out
pushing, pulling, hoisting, lifting the supplies onto
the continental divide. Up there, on the very top,
they made a house and rested while they got their

strength back. Then they started down for the sea, and the going down was as hard as the going up had been.

When at last they put their great timbers of bitter wood in the water to test them, they found that the sea worm attacked them just the same! They did not waste time complaining about the great effort they had made in vain, but immediately started cutting down trees on the Pacific coast. Nothing, not false starts, hunger, or hardships, would stop Balboa from achieving his goal. This time the ship timbers withstood the *broma*. When his first two ships were ready, he sailed them to the Pearl Islands, which he decided he would make his base for the main exploration to the south. And so, while the other two brigantines were being finished and additional supplies were being brought over from Acla, he sailed toward Peru. He had gone about one hundred miles when his ships were surrounded by a school of whales, sea monsters larger than the ships, that lashed and spouted and churned the sea into foam. Terrified, the sailors threw out their anchors. The frisking whales soon passed them and the sea grew calm. But then the wind changed, and they had to return to their base in the Pearl Islands.

That was as far as Balboa sailed. "A man," he said, "goes as far as he can and not as far as he wishes."

The rest of the story is swift and terrible.

When Balboa returned, a letter brought with the supplies from Acla informed him that a new governor had been appointed to replace Pedrarias. But Pedrarias knew that Balboa still had four ships ready and three hundred men willing to sail with him to Peru—the fabulous Peru where, outside Pedrarias's control, Balboa hoped to win fame and wealth. The very thought of this made Pedrarias vow that this last insult, this final humiliation to his pride and dreams, would never take place. While he still was governor he must move quickly, or he might never stop Balboa.

And so Pedrarias laid his plan. He invited Balboa to meet him in Acla, pretending he wanted to discuss supplies. Next, he arranged to have Pizarro, whom Balboa trusted, arrest him when he arrived at the mountain-top resthouse. The unsuspecting Balboa, certain of his innocence, deeply loyal to the law and the governor, meekly handed over his sword and allowed himself to be taken prisoner. As a prisoner, he was taken back to Acla. The trial was quick and secret, the verdict prearranged.

Balboa was charged with treason. He and he alone, the indictment read, had been responsible for refusing to allow Nicuesa to land and become the rightful governor of Darién. One of Enciso's old lies finally became, in the hands of Pedrarias, a kind of deadly, poisoned arrow. And the governor took no chance that the arrow might miss; he demanded that the judge find Balboa guilty.

The very next day—a date sometime between the 12th and 20th of January, 1519—Balboa was beheaded.

Fortunately his cruelly needless death was not the end of Balboa. Though Pedrarias after the beheading, his hatred still unspent, had ordered Balboa's head stuck on a pole as if he had been a common thief, the governor could not kill what Balboa had always valued more than his life—his achievements. The town crier announced that the *adelantado* of the South Sea had been executed for treason, but no one in Darién believed the charge. "What they call treason, no one took for such,"

remarked Oviedo, then a Darién official, when he later wrote the story of Darién.

The citizens knew that Balboa had signed his own death warrant when he built and equipped four ships. They also believed that Balboa had been put to death merely to allow Pedrarias to grab the ships. It was the only way Pedrarias could stop Balboa from sailing over the South Sea to the glory and gold of Peru.

Having eliminated his rival, Pedrarias lost no time in crossing the Isthmus along the road Balboa had hacked out of the wilderness while transporting the timbers and supplies for his seagoing boats. And then, hoping to expunge Balboa's name and deeds, Pedrarias took formal possession of "all the coast of the New Land and of the Sea of the South . . . with all its islands, ports, passages, coves, and creeks." His act, so base in motive, so futile in effect, was dated January 27, 1519. Two days later, having sailed to the Pearl Islands, he took special possession of them—how very special was proved by the huge fortune in pearls that fell into the governor's hands. One of the men who accompanied him and witnessed both these documents was Pizarro. Five years later he would lead the search

for the gold of the Incas. It was for this opportunity
that he had betrayed Balboa into Pedrarias's hands.

Pedrarias's acts of possession were duly recorded,
but they were not deemed worthy of remembrance.
Neither, for all his power and pearls, was Pedrarias
Dávila. And because he was not a murderer like
Pedrarias nor a thief like Pizarro, because in his
brief time the Spaniards held the friendship of
many Indian tribes, Balboa's years are a happy moment in the long tale of betrayal and butchery. It
is Vasco Nuñez de Balboa who rightly won lasting
fame, and who is honored today as the conqueror of
the cordilleras, trail blazer of the Isthmus, and discoverer of the Pacific.

Bibliography

For Source Material:

Andagoya, Pascual de, NARRATIVE OF THE PROCEEDINGS OF PEDRARIAS DÁVILA IN . . . TIERRA FIRME OR CASTILLA DEL ORO. Translated by C. F. Markham. London, Hakluyt Society, 1865.

Anderson, C. L. G., LIFE AND LETTERS OF VASCO NUÑEZ DE BALBOA. New York, Fleming H. Revell Company, 1941.
——— OLD PANAMA AND CASTILLA DEL ORO. Boston, L. C. Page & Co., 1914.

D'Anghera, Peter Martyr, DE ORBE NOVO. Translated from the Latin with Notes and Introduction by C. F. MacNutt. 2 vols. New York, G. P. Putnam's Sons, 1912.

Díaz del Castillo, Bernal, THE TRUE HISTORY OF THE CONQUEST OF NEW SPAIN. 4 vols. Edited by A. P. Maudslay. London, Hakluyt Society, second series, 1908–16.

Irving, Washington, VOYAGES AND DISCOVERIES OF THE COMPANIONS OF COLUMBUS. 3 vols. New York and London, Cooperative Publications Society, n. d.

WEBSTER'S SEVENTH NEW COLLEGIATE DICTIONARY. Springfield, Massachusetts, G. & C. Merriam Company, 1961.

For Background:

Bourne, Edward Gaylord, SPAIN IN AMERICA 1450–1580. New York, Harper and Brothers, 1906.

Clark, G. N., THE SEVENTEENTH CENTURY. Oxford, Clarendon Press, 1931.

Dobie, J. Frank, THE MUSTANGS. Boston, Little, Brown & Company, 1952.

Ghent, W. J., THE EARLY FAR WEST. A NARRATIVE OUTLINE,
1540–1850. New York and Toronto, Longmans, Green &
Company, 1931.

Humboldt, Alexander von, POLITICAL ESSAY ON THE KING-
DOM OF NEW SPAIN. Translated from the original French by
John Black. 2 vols. New York, I. Riley, 1811.

MacNutt, C. F., BARTHOLOMEW DE LAS CASAS: HIS LIFE, HIS
APOSTOLATE, AND HIS WRITINGS. New York, G. P. Putnam's
Sons, 1909.

Mattingly, Garrett, CATHERINE OF ARAGON. Boston, Little,
Brown & Company, 1941.

Merriman, R. B., THE RISE OF THE SPANISH EMPIRE IN THE
OLD WORLD AND IN THE NEW. 4 vols. New York, The
Macmillan Company, 1918–34.

Mirsky, Jeannette, THE WESTWARD CROSSINGS. New York,
Alfred A. Knopf, 1946.

Morison, Samuel Eliot, ADMIRAL OF THE OCEAN SEA. A LIFE
OF CHRISTOPHER COLUMBUS. 2 vols. Boston, Little, Brown
& Company, 1942.

Parr, Charles McKew, SO NOBLE A CAPTAIN; THE LIFE AND
TIMES OF FERDINAND MAGELLAN. New York, Crowell,
1963.

Prescott, William Hickling, HISTORY OF THE CONQUEST OF
MEXICO. 3 vols. New York, Harper and Brothers, 1843.

——— HISTORY OF THE REIGN OF FERDINAND AND ISABELLA,
THE CATHOLIC. 3 vols. Tenth edition. New York, Harper
and Brothers, 1845–6.

Priestley, Herbert Ingram, THE COMING OF THE WHITE MAN
1492–1848. New York, The Macmillan Company, 1930.

Simpson, Lesley Byrd, THE ENCOMIENDA IN NEW SPAIN; FORCED LABOR IN THE SPANISH COLONIES, 1492–1550. Berkeley, University of California Publications in History, Vol. 19, 1929.

Trend, J. B., THE CIVILIZATION OF SPAIN. New York and London, Oxford University Press, 1944.

Webb, Walter P., THE GREAT PLAINS. Boston, Ginn & Company, 1931.

Order of Events

August, 1492
–March, 1493

Christopher Columbus sets sail from Palos, Spain. He discovers islands off the coast of North America and leaves men to establish the settlement at La Navidad on the island of Hispaniola (now divided between Haiti and the Dominican Republic). Returns to Spain.

1493

The King and Queen of Spain give Columbus the title Admiral of the Ocean Sea. He is also made viceroy and governor-general of all lands he has discovered and all lands he may discover in the future. His titles are hereditary.

September, 1493–June, 1496

Returning to the New World on his second voyage with fifteen hundred colonists, Columbus finds La Navidad destroyed. In 1493 he establishes another settlement on Hispaniola and names it Isabella. But its location is unsatisfactory. A third settlement, Santo Domingo, is set up on the southern coast of the same island.

May, 1498

Columbus begins his third voyage. He explores a large portion of the north shore of South America and notices quantities of rich pearls on many of the Indians.

1500

Because of mismanagement and discontent on Hispaniola, Columbus is replaced as governor-general by Francisco de Bobadilla.

1501

Rodrigo de Bastidas sets out from Hispaniola and explores the shores of the Caribbean. Balboa ships on this voyage to the Pearl

Coast, which Columbus was told about but didn't explore. Bastidas collects great treasure in pearls and returns to Spain. Balboa begins his unsuccessful attempt to support himself as a farmer and adventurer on Hispaniola, and incurs debts which, by law, prevent him from leaving the island and furthering his fortunes on the mainland.

1502   Francisco de Bobadilla dies.
Nicolas de Ovando becomes governor of Hispaniola until 1509.

May, 1502–   Columbus makes his fourth and last voyage to
November,   the New World, tracing the coast of Central
1504   America—Veragua—from Bonacca Island, off Honduras, to the west shore of the Gulf of Darién, Colombia, called by the Indians the Gulf of Urabá.

1508   Alonso de Ojeda and Diego de Nicuesa each receive a ten-year commission from King Ferdinand to govern and colonize that vast stretch of the mainland, discovered by Bastidas and Columbus, from Veragua to the Pearl Coast. The Gulf of Urabá is the boundary separating them.

1509   Diego Colón, Christopher Columbus's son, becomes governor of Hispaniola.

1510   After the opposition of Diego Colón is overcome, the expeditions of Ojeda and Nicuesa finally leave Hispaniola. Ojeda's supply ships, under the command of Martín de Enciso, are scheduled to leave two months after Ojeda's main party.

A large number of Ojeda's men are killed by Indians at the site of present-day Cartagena, Colombia. The expedition moves farther west along the coast and founds a colony at San Sebastián on the Gulf of Urabá.

In the meantime, Nicuesa's ships have foundered off the coast of Panama. The survivors establish a colony in a deserted Indian village, which they christen Nombre de Dios.

After Enciso's supply ships founder near San Sebastián, Balboa, who has stowed away aboard ship, rallies the men and leads them to an Indian village on the western shore of the Gulf of Urabá. They capture the village and name it Santa María de la Antigua del Darién.

The colonists deprive Enciso of his authority. The mayoralty is shared by Balboa and Martín de Zamudio.

Nicuesa is forbidden to land at Santa María de la Antigua, which lies within his grant. However, his followers are welcomed. Nicuesa sails away to an unknown fate.

April, 1511   At Balboa's suggestion, Enciso, Zamudio, and Juan de Valdivia are sent as envoys to the governor of Hispaniola and to King Ferdinand. Valdivia is to return from Hispaniola with supplies for the colony.

In Spain Enciso represents Balboa to be an upstart and traitor. Zamudio defends Balboa but falls out of favor with the powerful Bishop Fonseca and must go into hiding.

Balboa captures the chief Careta, then makes him an ally. The Indians pledge themselves to help the colonists raise crops, to act as guides, and to serve as interpreters in dealing with other tribes.

Balboa makes an alliance with Comogre, whose eldest son tells Balboa of a great ocean on the other side of the Isthmus of Panama.

November, 1512

Balboa sends Rodrigo de Colmenares and Juan de Quecido to report the success of Darién to the governor of Hispaniola and to King Ferdinand. They are to request supplies from Hispaniola and report the existence of an unknown sea to the king.

Balboa receives a letter from King Ferdinand appointing him temporary governor and acting captain general of the Province of Darién. He also receives a letter from Zamudio, who is still in hiding, in which he is warned that Bishop Fonseca plans his downfall. Balboa decides to begin his march to the South Sea without further delay.

May, 1513

In spite of Colmenares' favorable report on Balboa, Bishop Fonseca determines to make Pedrarias Dávila governor of Darién.

July, 1513

Pedrarias Dávila is commissioned by the king (at Fonseca's request) as governor of the

Province of Darién, which, since the arrival of Colmenares and his news of great treasure and the existence of the South Sea, has been renamed Castilla del Oro.

September, 1513

Balboa and his men begin their march to the southern coast of Darién.

September 25, 1513

From a peak in the mountains, Balboa sights the South Sea.

September 29, 1513

On the Bay of San Miguel, Balboa formally claims the South Sea for Spain.

Instead of returning directly to Darién, Balboa explores additional territory and conquers the powerful chief Tubanamá. He amasses great treasure in gold and pearls.

January, 1514

Upon Balboa's return to Darién, Pedro de Arbolancha, a secret agent of the king, observes the scrupulously fair division of treasure and the efficient operation of the colony.

April 14, 1514

Pedrarias Dávila begins his expedition to Castilla del Oro (Darién) with fifteen ships and two thousand men.

Arbolancha gives his favorable report to the King, who makes Balboa governor of the coast of the South Sea. This territory is still under the jurisdiction of the governor of Darién, Pedrarias Dávila.

July, 1514

Pedrarias Dávila arrives in Darién with his new colonists. On hearing of Balboa's discovery of the South Sea, Pedrarias, who had hoped to perform this exploit himself, vows to punish Balboa. Most of the two thousand men die of fever or return to Hispaniola.

1516   Ferdinand II dies. His grandson, Charles, becomes king of Spain.

1516–1519   Planning the conquest of Peru, Balboa builds ships and sails to the Pearl Islands. From there he starts for Peru, but shifting winds force him to turn back.

January, 1519   Learning of Balboa's plans, Pedrarias Dávila decides to stop him once and for all. He recalls Balboa on a pretext of business and has him arrested on the charge of treason. Pedrarias forces the judge to find Balboa guilty. Balboa is executed.

Dramatis Personae

JERÓNIMO DE AGUILAR: A Franciscan monk who traveled on the ship sent from the colony of Darién to Hispaniola in January, 1512, under the command of Juan de Valdivia. The ship sank on the way to Hispaniola, and Brother Aguilar was one of the survivors. Captured by cannibals, he escaped and was adopted by a friendly tribe. In 1519 he became one of Cortés's interpreters in the conquest of Mexico.

DIEGO DE ALMAGRO (1475–1538): One of the soldiers who came to Darién from Spain, in the expedition of Pedrarias Dávila, who was appointed governor of Darién in 1513. Almagro aided Pizarro in the conquest of Peru in 1532.

PEDRO DE ARBOLANCHA: A confidential agent of King Ferdinand who was sent to Darién in 1514 to ascertain whether or not Balboa, as temporary governor of Darién, was ruling fairly.

PEDRO ARIAS DE ÁVILA (Pedrarias Dávila, 1440–1531?): A polished courtier and a favorite of the influential Bishop Fonseca, who persuaded King Ferdinand to appoint Pedrarias governor of Darién. Dávila became a dangerous enemy of Balboa's.

RODRIGO DE BASTIDAS (1460–1526): A lawyer who led an expedition to explore the coast of present-day Colombia in 1501. Among his crew were Balboa and Juan de la Cosa. Bastidas took great stores of pearls and treasure from the Indians, all of which he kept to himself.

SEBASTIÁN DE BELALCÁZAR (1479–1551): He accompanied Christopher Columbus on his third voyage to the New World (1498) and came to Darién with Pedrarias Dávila in 1514. In

1532 he was with Pizarro during the conquest of Peru. In 1533 he took the Indian stronghold at Quito, Ecuador, and in 1535 he captured Popayán (Southwest Colombia).

FRANCISCO DE BOBADILLA (?–1502): An able administrator sent by King Ferdinand and Queen Isabella to replace Columbus as governor of Hispaniola in 1500.

JOHN CABOT (1461–1498): Under the sponsorship of Henry VII of England, he discovered the northeast coast of North America in 1497. All English claims to North America were to be based upon his discovery.

CARETA: The chief of one of the Indian tribes in Darién. Conquered by Balboa in a surprise raid, he became Balboa's first Indian friend as well as his ally and father-in-law.

CARLOS: The Christian name given to the eldest son of Comogre, an Indian chief. He first told Balboa of the existence of the South Sea and the fabulously wealthy kingdom of Tubanamá.

CÉMACO: The chief of the tribe which had occupied the village Balboa renamed Santa María de la Antigua del Darién. After being driven from the village, Cémaco became a steadfast enemy of Balboa's.

CHARLES V (1500–1558): Son of Juana of Castile and Philip I and grandson of Ferdinand and Isabella. He inherited the throne of Spain, as Charles I, in 1516 and became Holy Roman Emperor Charles V in 1519.

CHIAPES: One of the tribal chiefs whom Balboa conquered and befriended after the discovery of the South Sea.

RODRIGO DE COLMENARES: The man commissioned by Diego de Nicuesa to bring extra supply ships to the colony which

Nicuesa hoped to found on the present-day Isthmus of Panama. Colmenares later deserted Nicuesa and joined Balboa's colony.

DON DIEGO COLÓN (1472–1526): Son of Christopher Columbus. He inherited, through Ferdinand and Isabella's agreement with his father, the governorship of Hispaniola in 1509.

CHRISTOPHER COLUMBUS (1451–1506): Referred to by the Spaniards as Cristobal Colón. His namesake, Saint Christopher, is said to have borne the Christ Child across a river on his back; Columbus believed that he, in the manner of his patron saint, was destined to bear Christianity across the ocean to new lands. On October 12, 1492, he landed on Watling Island (San Sálvador) in the Bahamas. On his first voyage he also discovered and claimed for Spain the islands of Cuba and Hispaniola. By his contract with Ferdinand and Isabella he became governor-general of all the new lands he had discovered and would discover in the New World. In 1500, because of reports that Columbus's colony on Hispaniola was being mismanaged, Ferdinand and Isabella replaced him with a new governor, named Bobadilla. That same year Bobadilla sent Columbus back to Spain in chains, but Columbus was released as soon as he arrived. In all, he made four voyages to America, discovering many more islands in the Caribbean and exploring the coasts of present-day Nicaragua, Panama, Costa Rica, Colombia, and Venezuela.

COMOGRE: One of the first Indian chiefs befriended by Balboa. He gave the conquistador large amounts of gold as well as guides to accompany the Spaniards to the South Sea.

FRANCISCO VASQUEZ DE CORONADO (1510–1554): A governor of Mexico who set out, in 1540, to discover the legendary

Seven Cities of Cíbola. Although his expedition found no gold, it opened the present-day American Southwest.

CORRAL: One of the colonists at Darién, a lawyer who unsuccessfully plotted to overthrow Balboa.

HERNANDO CORTÉS (1485–1547): The conquistador who overthrew the Aztec empire of Moctezuma in Mexico in 1519.

JUAN DE LA COSA (1460–1510): Owner and pilot of Columbus's flagship *Santa María* in 1492 and pilot for Rodrigo de Bastidas during the latter's expedition of 1501. He was killed by Indians at the start of Alonso de Ojeda's expedition of 1510, leaving Balboa as the only man on that expedition with the knowledge of Indian customs necessary for the Spaniards' survival.

PEDRARIAS DÁVILA: *See* Arias de Ávila.

BERNAL DÍAZ DEL CASTILLO (1492–1581): One of the colonists who came to Darién with Pedrarias Dávila in 1514. In 1519 he was with Cortés during the conquest of Mexico. In his destitute old age he wrote the fascinating classic *The True History of the Conquest of New Spain*.

DITES: The chief who ruled the Pearl Islands when Balboa visited them in 1514.

MARTÍN FERNANDEZ DE ENCISO (?–1519): A wealthy attorney who financed Alonso de Ojeda's expedition of 1510 in exchange for being the mayor in the colony which Ojeda had been commissioned to establish in the New World.

FERDINAND II (1452–1516): King of Aragon, who ruled Spain jointly with his wife, Queen Isabella of Castile.

BISHOP JUAN RODRIGUEZ DE FONSECA (1451–1524): King Ferdinand's highly influential advisor, who until 1503 was solely responsible for planning and regulating voyages to the New World. After 1499 the volume of colonial business became very great. In 1503 Fonseca helped to organize the Casa de Contratación de las Indias (the House of Trade of the Indies) which began as an institution for fostering and supervising colonial trade but which soon became an all-embracing ministry of colonial affairs. Fonseca still retained his influence and used it to control the policies of the Casa de Contratación. The enterprises of Columbus, Balboa, and Cortés were greatly hampered by Fonseca's efforts to award control of the newly discovered lands to his political favorites at the Spanish court. In 1514, when the Casa de Contratación sent two thousand new colonists to Darién, Pedrarias Dávila, a favorite of Fonseca's, headed the expedition as the colony's new governor.

ISABELLA I (1451–1504): Wife of Ferdinand II of Aragon and Queen of Castile and Leon. She was an energetic and able administrator and a fervent Christian. In 1492, after the Moors had been driven out of Granada, she ordered all Jews banished from Spain. As a result the port of Cadiz was so crowded with refugee ships that Columbus's first expedition, which Isabella sponsored, had to leave from the relatively obscure port of Palos.

JUANA LA LOCA (Joanna the Mad, 1479–1555): She assumed the regency of Castile and Leon after the death of her mother, Queen Isabella, in 1504. By 1507 she had advanced so far into insanity that her father, King Ferdinand, took the regency from her. Her son, Charles, became king of Spain in 1516, three years before Balboa's death.

FERDINAND MAGELLAN (1480–1521): In 1519, sponsored by King Charles of Spain, he led an expedition to find a westward route to the Molucca Islands. Sailing down the coast of South

America, he discovered the Straits of Magellan, through which he sailed to the South Sea. He renamed the ocean "Pacific." Although Magellan was killed in the Philippines, one of his ships, the *Victoria,* reached Spain in 1522: the first to sail around the globe.

MOCTEZUMA (1480–1520): The emperor of the Aztec Empire of Mexico, conquered by Cortés in 1519.

DIEGO DE NICUESA (?–1511): A courtier to whom King Ferdinand gave a ten-year commission in 1508 to explore the coast of Panama and Central America and to establish at least one colony there. His grant extended from the Gulf of Urabá west to the cape called Gracias a Dios.

PERALONSO NIÑO: A Spanish explorer who had sailed with Columbus on two of the latter's four voyages. Around 1501 he explored the South American coast and returned to Spain with a huge fortune in pearls.

ALONSO DE OJEDA (1466–1515?): In 1508 King Ferdinand gave him a ten-year commission to explore and colonize the section of the Pearl Coast lying east of the Gulf of Urabá and west of Cabo de la Vela. He and Nicuesa, having received their commissions and started their expeditions at the same time, were bitter rivals.

GONZALO FERNANDEZ OVIEDO: A notary and official in charge of smelting and marking gold, who was a member of Pedrarias Dávila's expedition to Darién in 1514. He became one of the first historians of the New World.

FRANCISCO PIZARRO (1476–1541): An illiterate swineherd, Pizarro served as a common soldier with Ojeda and Balboa. He conquered the Inca empire of Peru in 1532.

POCOROSA: One of the Indian chiefs befriended by Balboa

after the discovery of the South Sea. Pocorosa's warriors helped Balboa capture Tubanamá.

PONCA: An Indian chief and an elusive enemy of Balboa's who was persuaded to become an ally.

QUAREQUÁ (?–1513): The powerful chief who ruled the mountains from which Balboa had his first view of the South Sea. One of the most feared rulers on the Isthmus, he and his warriors were easily slaughtered by Spanish steel and gunpowder.

JUAN DE QUECIDO: The elderly colonist who, with Rodrigo de Colmenares, left Darién for Spain in 1512 in order to announce Balboa's intention of searching for the South Sea.

RUA: The Darién colonist who joined the lawyer Corral in an unsuccessful attempt to overthrow Balboa.

JUAN SERRANO (?–1521): The chief pilot of Pedrarias Dávila's fleet, which sailed to Darién in 1514. A few years later he sailed with Magellan and died alongside of his commander in the Philippines.

HERNANDO DE SOTO (1500–1542): After serving under Pedrarias Dávila in Darién, he fought under Pizarro during the conquest of Peru. Named adelantado of Florida by King Charles of Spain, he landed on the Florida coast in 1539 and began explorations that reached halfway across the continent of North America. In 1542 he discovered the Mississippi River and died of wounds received during a fight with Indians.

TEOCA: Another Indian chief befriended by Balboa after the discovery of the South Sea.

JUAN DE VALDIVIA (?–1512): An elderly colonist who was twice sent by Balboa to request additional supplies from Don

Diego Colón, the governor of Hispaniola. On his second voyage to Hispaniola in 1512 a storm destroyed his ship. He perished and only eight passengers survived, Brother Aguilar among them.

AMERIGO VESPUCCI (1454–1512): A Florentine merchant who went to Spain in the service of the powerful Medici family of Italy. Trained in navigational sciences, he sailed in the expedition of Alonso de Ojeda in 1499. Leaving the expedition before land was sighted, Vespucci's ship went on alone to discover the mouths of the Amazon River. In 1501, for the Portuguese, he explored six thousand miles of the coast of South America and took the first measurements to determine the exact longitude (or east-west position) of the new land mass. By these calculations he was convinced that Columbus had discovered a new continent, completely separate from Asia. His letters to friends, in which he explained his theories, were published in Europe and widely read. In this way his name became closely associated with the New World. In 1507, with the publication of Martin Waldseemüller's book entitled *Cosmographiae Introductio*, the New World was called "America" for the first time, in Vespucci's honor.

MARTÍN DE ZAMUDIO: The colonist who was elected co-mayor with Balboa after Enciso antagonized the colonists at Darién and was deposed. When he was sent to the court of Spain as the colony's representative, Zamudio fiercely defended Balboa against Enciso's slander. Bishop Fonseca took a dislike to Zamudio, who had to go into hiding.

Index

Magellan, Ferdinand, 41, 125, 157–58
Martinique, 8
Moctezuma, 65, 156, 158
Moors, 5, 130, 157

Nicuesa, Diego de, 14, 16–17, 24, 33–36, 48–49, 61, 68, 72–73, 75, 77, 130, 140, 148–49, 154 158
Niño, Peralonso, 10
Nombre de Dios, 34, 36, 48–49, 60, 149

Ojeda, Alonso de, 14, **15**, 16–18, 21–24, 26–28, 36–37, 61, 73, 75, 77, 130, 148–49, 156, 158
Ovando, Nicholas de, 148
Oviedo, Gonzalo Fernandez, 125, 141–42, 158

Pacific Ocean, 4, **30**, 86, **97**, 98, 100, 143; claimed by Balboa for Spain, 102–3; named, 158; see also South Sea
Panama, Isthmus of, 4, 10, 14, **30**, 33, 42, 44, 90, 142–43, 149–50, 154; first crossing of, **89**, 103
Pearl Coast, 10, 20–22, 24, 147–48
Pearl Islands, **30**, 136, 139, 142, 152, 156

Peru, 27, 85, 106, 112, 125, 138–39, 142, 152, 158
Pizarro, Francisco, 27–28, 35, 85, 106, 111–12, 125, 139, 142–43, 153–54, 158
Pocorosa, 109–11, 158–59
Ponca, 53, 88–89, 91, 94, 100, 107, 159
Puerto Rico, 8

Quarequá, 56–58, 83, 90–94, **93**, 99, 107, 111, 159
Quecido, Juan de, 70–71, 75, 150, 159

Rua, 68–69, 115, 159

San Miguel, Bay of, **30**, **101**, 103, 151
San Sebastián, 26–29, 60, 149
Santa María, 39
Santa María de la Antigua del Darién, **30**, 33–34, 36, 38, 149, 154; see also Darién
Santo Domingo, 8–9, 11–12, 16–17, 20, 24, 27, 71, 147
Serrano, Juan, 125, 159
Seville, 128
Seville Cathedral, 14, 15
Sierra of Quarequá, **30**, 95, **97**
Soto, Hernando de, 124–25, 159
South Sea, **30**, 56, 62, 73, 75, 78–79, 84, 90, 95–96, 98–99, 104, 119, 128, 135–37, 142,